Mr. Father

Mr. Father

Father Mike Bassano's Global Quest
for Spiritual Authenticity

BY MICHAEL P. MCNALLY

To view pictures and to order this book: go to fathermikebook.com.

Become a fan of *Mr. Father* on Facebook by typing in "Mike Bassano" in the search bar.

Library of Congress Control Number: 2011914222

ISBN: 978-1-60126-299-8

For Mary Josephine and Anne Rose

An ounce of mother is worth a pound of clergy.

— Spanish Proverb

When your ship, long moored in harbor, gives you the illusion of being a house — put out to sea! Save your boat's journeying soul, and your own pilgrim soul, cost what it may.

— *Brazilian Bishop Dom Hélder Câmara*

It is not our job to convert anyone. That is God's business.

— *Mother Teresa*

CONTENTS

Author's Note

In the early stages of this project, Father Mike, his family, friends, colleagues, and those he encountered throughout his life, provided me with troves of remarkable memories. The first drafts of *Mr. Father* were an accumulation of practically every event and detail I had amassed during research. I thought, at the time, my initial efforts were commendable. Thankfully, others disagreed. I was under the false impression that in order to tell Father Mike's story, I had to include all of his experiences, however inconsequential. I was attempting to share a story of spiritual growth, while at the same time trying to adhere to an historical biography model.

Then I came across the book *Night*, by Elie Wiesel. In just over a hundred pages, Wiesel captures the horror of barely surviving the Nazi concentration camps of Buchenwald and Auschwitz. In interviews Wiesel gave in the decades following its release, he explained that the original draft of *Night* was 892 pages. Under pressure from his editor, he reluctantly cut the text down to its publication length. After letting go of almost 800 pages, Wiesel felt the shorter version, surprisingly, carried the same impact of his first draft.

My initial drafts of *Mr. Father* weren't nearly as long as Wiesel's, but I realized I had to make significant cuts to serve the story. Some of what I took out was superfluous and easy to shelve. Other parts I had grown attached to, taking me the better part of a year to finally hit the delete key. Once these facets were gone, the essential elements and prevailing themes of Father Mike's life surfaced. Elie Wiesel was right.

What follows is a narrative nonfiction account of Father Mike's life, highlighting his spiritual growth. Some names have been changed for the sake of anonymity, and when necessary, direct quotes have been condensed or adjusted for grammar and clarity — *while at no time changing the contributor's original intent*. Recollections via extensive interviews are the basis for dialogue. I do not interject myself into the story until the last chapter, where I refer to myself as *a friend* and *Anne's son*, so as not to break from the narrative employed in the rest of the book.

After Father Mike read and gave his blessing to disclose the content of this book, he asked me to emphasize to the reader that in anyone's life, disagreements are inevitable and essential for growth to occur. He also wished to convey that his opinions, though greatly influenced by his experiences as a Maryknoller, are not necessarily a reflection of views held by other Maryknollers or Maryknoll as an organization.

I have known Father Mike for thirty years. He is my friend. In researching and writing this book, I have gone to great lengths to remain fair and objective. Still, I would be remiss to say that I'm an impartial biographer. I find Father Mike's commitment to humanity inspiring. I hope you do too.

Michael P. McNally
Buffalo
June 2011

INTRODUCTION
FRANCE — FEBRUARY 2008

Father Mike Bassano walked into Le Laboratoire Gallery in the heart of Paris. Photo journalist James Nachtwey, of *Time* and *National Geographic* fame, had invited Mike to his exhibition entitled *Struggle for Life*. The gallery walls were lined with photographs displaying the calamitous impact of AIDS, tuberculosis, and malaria on the third world. Nineteen of the black and white images were of Mike at work.

A few years earlier, Nachtwey happened upon Mike at a Buddhist AIDS hospice on the grounds of Prabhat Namphu Temple, north of Bangkok, Thailand. Mike was going about his daily routine of bathing, feeding, and changing the diapers of emaciated and sore covered patients — victims of a viral holocaust.

MR. FATHER

Khoon Pauw (Mr. Father), as the patients referred to Mike, was one of the few people who still cared about their needs. The vast majority of patients had been dropped off at the temple by family members who would never return. The stigma of having AIDS in Thailand brought shame and dishonor to families, regardless of how the disease was contracted. In the days and months the forgotten held onto life, Mike watered their parched throats and tended to their lesions. When their hearts stopped beating, he carried their bodies to the temple's crematoriums for incineration. Then he went back to work.

A few days after the exhibition in France, *Paris Match Online* featured a story about Mike entitled *A Christian Saint Living Amongst the Untouchables of Thailand*. It made the priest uncomfortable. Mike had no aspirations of any label other than servant. He had come to Paris to tell the remarkable stories of resilience he had witnessed during his four years at the temple.

This wasn't the first time he had been placed on a pedestal by people searching for a living embodiment of the divine. Throughout his life, many believed Mike had been endowed with gifts beyond themselves. Yet it wasn't that simple.

Introduction

Mike Bassano was born into a pivotal age. Over the last century, as technological advances have made the world smaller, people of all faiths have been torn between institutional religious norms and progressive notions of spirituality. Mike has often been referred to as a "living saint", but the events of his life and the struggles he has faced embody the inner-turmoil of a generation thrust into globalization. How does one embrace an expanding definition of the divine and still value tradition? For Mike Bassano, the answer comes in one word.

"Compassion. It unites us and makes us whole. It melts away all barriers — religious, ethnic, or otherwise. Compassion opens us up to a heaven...here and now."

PART ONE

The Journey Outward

one

THE CALLING
MEXICO CITY — 1985

"Romero!" an elderly Salvadoran woman exclaimed, as if she were staring at a ghost.

"Si, Romero," her husband concurred.

Mike Bassano bore an uncanny resemblance to the martyred El Salvadoran Archbishop. Oscar Romero had been gunned down five years earlier for standing up to injustices committed by a ruthless military regime in his small Central American country. Mike was not in El Salvador that spring day though. He was in the slums of Mexico City, where thousands of Salvadorans had sought refuge from their country's bloody civil war.

The GATE Program (Global Awareness Through Experience) was Mike's reason for being in the Mexican capital.

GATE exposed individuals from various denominations to the realities of third world populations. Participants also attended seminars led by sociologists and theologians, gaining insight into the causes of the poverty that surrounded them.

Mike had chosen to attend GATE for a couple reasons. As a Catholic priest, continuing education was always encouraged by his home diocese in Upstate New York. Yet Mike's presence in the Mexican slums was more about a profound summons he'd experienced eighteen months earlier.

UTICA, NEW YORK — 1984

Mike made no commitments to spend New Year's Day with friends or family. He planned on relaxing in his bedroom on the third floor of Historic St. John's rectory. He looked forward to reading, making a few phone calls, and enjoying some time to himself. December is for priests what April is for accountants. A day of rest and solitude after Advent was a welcomed respite for the priest.

Following 11 a.m. Mass, Mike chatted with parishioners as he meandered back to the church's sacristy. He intended on meeting Deacon Bill Dischiavo and Pastor John Flanagan at a local diner for brunch. He hung his stole in the closet. The altar boys scurried out before he could wish them a Happy New Year. Then, alone in the church, the call came.

"I heard a clear voice inside me say, '*Go to Maryknoll*,'" Mike remembers.

There were no hovering apparitions or rays of light shining through the church's windows. The call had come from within. It was undeniable and he knew he would follow it.

"We usually took a few days off after the holidays anyway," Mike recalls. "So at brunch, I told John Flanagan I was going out of town. He didn't ask me where I was going and I didn't tell him. I wasn't trying to hide anything, but I thought it best to keep it to myself."

After digging up a few newspaper articles he'd held onto about the Maryknoll Society, Mike took out a road atlas and charted a course to Ossining, New York.

Mike had heard of Maryknoll years earlier. For Catholic clergy in the U.S., Maryknoll was known as the chief mission sending society of the American Council of Bishops. Maryknoll showed up on Mike's radar in December of 1980. The society was thrust into the international spotlight that year when two of its missioners stationed in El Salvador, Sisters Ita Ford and Maura Clarke (along with lay missioner Jean Donovan and Ursuline nun Dorothy Kazel), were raped, shot, and buried in shallow graves after being pulled over by plain-clothed Salvadoran national guardsmen. Prior to their deaths, the Maryknoll nuns had been active in finding medical attention and shelter for Salvadorans displaced by violent civil strife. The nuns' actions were seen as an affront to the military junta in power. It was later revealed that the guardsmen responsible for their deaths were not only acting on orders from their commanding officer, but had also been trained by the U.S. Department of Defense.

El Salvador was home to one of many dictatorships that came to power in Latin America during the second half of the twentieth century. The military regimes that reigned in El Salvador, Argentina, Chile, Uruguay, Paraguay, Bolivia and Brazil were merciless human rights violators.

The School of the Americas (SOA), now called The Western Hemisphere Institute for Security Cooperation, was a training facility in Fort Benning, Georgia run by the U.S. Department of Defense. Since 1946, U.S. sanctioned authoritarian regimes had sent their soldiers to SOA to learn how to extort, torture, and execute individuals that threatened to disrupt U.S. corporate interests. The murders of the missioners had been foreshadowed eight months earlier when the Archbishop of San Salvador, Oscar Romero, was shot and killed on the altar by an SOA trained agent. Symbolizing righteous defiance, Romero and the nuns became icons of justice for Catholic laity and clergy throughout Latin America.

"I took notice and was intrigued by their bravery," Mike recalls. "I asked myself, 'Why would they put their lives at risk?' For the first time, I began to view service from a world perspective. Still, I had all intentions of spending the rest of my life in the Syracuse Diocese."

A loose tether had tied the deaths of Romero and the Maryknoll martyrs to Mike's diocesan ministry. He had not put himself in the middle of a civil war, but he had begun to see how the story of his childhood hero was central to the lives of his Puerto Rican parishioners.

"The story of Jesus' perseverance was something they used to get through the day," Mike recalls. "It wasn't just about going to church or praying. Their faith in what Jesus represented was a way of identifying with a world that hadn't given them much."

Mike and John Flanagan had taken Spanish classes as a way of connecting with the growing Puerto Rican population in Utica. In years past, they had conducted Masses in Spanish, but they didn't understand much of what they were saying.

"We were basically just reading an English-to-Spanish translation of the Liturgy," Mike recalls. "We felt that in order to really connect with them, we needed to learn the language."

Fluency in Spanish would come years later, but being able

to understand the basics, Mike was able to comprehend their struggles.

"These were poor families that made their living doing manual labor," Mike recalls. "I saw the discrimination they faced on a daily basis. At that point in my life, I felt sadness for them. I saw myself as someone who could provide comfort. I thought that was how I fit into their lives."

On the morning of January 2, 1984, Mike drove down the New York State Thruway through the snow covered Catskill Mountains. He pulled off the highway and made his way along the hilly roads of the Hudson Valley. He saw a sign with an arrow indicating that Maryknoll was just up the road. As the priest approached the Society's campus, a gargantuan mass of field stone jutted out from the hilltop horizon. The Asian styled roofing of the Society's main building conjured images of Buddhist temples he had seen only in photographs. Engraved above the building's archway was the Society's Latin motto, *Euntes Docete Omnes Gentes* (Go Out and Teach All Nations).

"It was hard not to feel that I was entering into a different world," Mike recalls.

Mike had not called Maryknoll ahead of time to notify anyone that he was coming.

"I just held my breath and said, 'I came all this way, I'm going in.'"

In 1911, Maryknoll was established by the Archbishops of the United States as the Catholic Foreign Mission Society of America. Prior to 1911, the United States was considered a mission-receiving country by the Vatican. With the advent of Maryknoll, U.S. Catholics could now send forth their own missioners. In the early twentieth century, Maryknoll founders, Father James Walsh and Father Thomas Price, trained missioners to convert foreign populations and establish Catholic communities abroad. The "convert the pagan babies of China" approach first practiced by Maryknollers evolved following Vatican II. In the mid-sixties, the Society began to work in the realms of social justice and interreligious dialogue.

"For the first time, the Church recognized God working in other cultures and faiths," Maryknoll historian, Father Michael Walsh, says. "This shifted the focus of our mission work away from just racking up numbers through conversion. After Vatican II, relationships with other religions began with an attitude of respect, as opposed to the earlier idea of going into cultures and replacing everything. Empowerment became fundamental to our approach."

MR. FATHER

A 1981 *Time* magazine article reported, "...starting with a 1966 policy statement, the Society (Maryknoll) also began emphasizing the need for change in social systems and the rallying of oppressed groups to demand their civil and economic rights. One priest explains the shift: 'The church is no longer only involved in giving the campesinos (farmers) plows and tools, but in making them conscious of their situation.'"

It was during this period that Maryknollers did away with traditional Catholic garb.

"We felt that collars and habits condemned our missioners to a narrowly defined role in other cultures," Walsh says. "We were now working on initiatives outside the institution, but still in the spirit of the Gospels."

Mike walked into the foyer of Maryknoll's main building and stood before a woman at the information desk.

"My name is Father Mike Bassano. I just drove down here from Utica and was wondering if I could talk to someone."

"Well, who do you want to speak with?"

"Umm...anyone."

The receptionist spotted Bob Sheridan, a husky Irish priest, across the room and called him over.

"Bob, this is Mike Bassano," The receptionist said. "Could you answer some questions for him?"

"What can I do for you Mike?" Bob asked.

"This is my first time here and I just wanted some information about what you guys do."

Bob looked at his watch. "It's lunchtime, Mike. Why don't you join me for some grub?"

Mike followed Bob downstairs to the cafeteria, telling him a little bit about himself. They grabbed some food and sat down at a table with six other clergymen. Bob made introductions.

"This is John, he just got back from Taiwan...James, he spent fifteen years in Tanzania...Jose was stationed in Peru."

Mike was in awe.

"I just sat there. These guys had spent most of their lives living in far off places. I was just Mike Bassano from Binghamton, New York. The furthest south I'd ever gone was Florida—for vacation."

As he listened to the missioners' stories of working in countries where famine and poverty were a way of life, he was both intimidated and fascinated.

"So Mike," one of the clergymen asked, "what brought you down here?"

"I'm not sure. I had heard about the place and wanted to learn more."

For the moment, Mike let logistical hurdles and self

doubt get the better of him. He had committed himself to the Syracuse Diocese for life. All of these men went into the seminary knowing they would spend their lives serving abroad. Most of them had been ordained by Maryknoll. It was a nice drive though and he met some interesting guys. Perhaps the call he had heard did not bear the significance he had hoped it would.

"Have I got the perfect thing for you, Mike," Bob Sheridan said. "You can still remain a diocesan priest and have an overseas experience with Maryknoll. You can be an associate missioner. All you have to do is fill out the paperwork and go through a discernment phase, where we'll see if we're a good fit. Then you just get approval from your Bishop to take a leave for five years."

Sheridan made it all sound so simple.

"Am I capable of this? Five years? Ask the Bishop?" Mike remembers thinking.

"So are you interested?" Sheridan asked.

"I'm not sure. Can I talk to the person in charge of the program?"

Sheridan took Mike to see Father Del Goodman.

"I explained to Del that I was happy in diocesan life," Mike recalls. "I felt a strong connection and loyalty to where I had come from. He was reassuring. He kept emphasizing that I wouldn't have to leave the diocese forever. "

Although Mike was concerned about what his colleagues and family might think, he felt that he was being carried into a new awareness. At the time, the idea of venturing off to another country was abstract. He wasn't about to jump ship and go half way around the world to save a starving child. Yet the experience of just being around those who had offered themselves up to the unknown had resonated with him.

Mike returned to Utica the next day. He told no one that he was even considering Maryknoll's offer. For the next year and a half, Mike continued fulfilling the needs of his parish. He corresponded with Maryknoll, but made no commitments. In early 1985, he did some research and recognized the GATE program as a good testing ground for his overseas inclinations.

"I didn't share with anyone where I thought this was leading me," Mike recalls. "I told my friends that it was just part of my continuing education."

Remaining silent allowed events to unfold without the short-lived propulsion of peer approval or the self-doubting effect of skepticism. Mike knew from his childhood that he needed to protect his callings. They were sacred. Outside chatter only fogged the path ahead. When, and if, the time came, he would seek guidance and even approval, but not just yet.

Mike registered to attend GATE in May of 1985. When he arrived in Mexico City the following month, he didn't know what to expect. The two weeks Mike spent there changed him forever. GATE organizers spoke of injustice and how they felt clergy must be on the side of the poor, no longer remaining apathetic to the atrocities occurring in Latin America. Observing poverty on a large scale, Mike's comprehension of third world needs solidified.

"I cried when the plane took off to go back home," Mike recalls. "I knew this was where I belonged—among those who had nothing."

When he returned to Historic St. John's, he found it hard to readjust. He had only been in Mexico briefly, but he could no longer deny he was being led.

"After GATE, I thought, *'How can I live like this? I sleep in a big warm rectory where all my meals are cooked for me.'* After all I had seen, I felt very uncomfortable."

He now believed he was ready to make the next step. The germination of his call came to fruition in the form of a letter to Bishop Frank Harrison. It was a letter, only eighteen months earlier, he had shuttered at the thought of writing.

"I had to act and act soon," Mike remembers. "I knew that feeling uncomfortable would turn into unhappiness. I didn't want to go down that road."

14

Mike worked on the letter for a couple weeks. He wanted to make sure every word was right. Mike asked to be released from the diocese for five years. He conveyed his feeling of loyalty and that it was not a spur-of-the moment decision. He described how he felt his work in Utica had been a preparation for a life abroad.

"When I finished writing it," Mike recalls, "I put it in an envelope, and set it up on my book shelf. I let it sit there for a week. I was concerned about what people would think. After tiring myself from worry, I just put it in the mail and said 'Here we go.'"

Mike received word in September of 1985 that Bishop Frank Harrison wished to meet with him to discuss his request. Driving down to Syracuse from Utica, he practiced his pitch to the Bishop.

"I tried to remember that each time I tested the boundaries of my self-doubt, I had grown as a person," Mike recalls.

Harrison listened as Mike made his case. When he finished, Harrison said, "I know there is a need for you here. We are definitely short on priests, but you have gifts Mike. I have seen them and heard about them. I think this is a good idea."

"My heart started pounding from fear and excitement," Mike recalls. "I felt I had been led to this moment since childhood."

15

two

MICKEY MANTLE AND JESUS
BINGHAMTON, NEW YORK — 1950s

On Tuesday afternoons, the pagans and Christians went to war on the south side of Binghamton. The students of St. John the Evangelist Parochial School strolled down one side of Vestal Avenue with an elated sense of freedom. The Abraham Lincoln Elementary School children walked down the other side of the street with a feeling of impending obligation. Tuesday was the day that St. John's kids were let out early from school so their teachers, mostly nuns, could instruct the public school children on the Catholic tradition.

Virtually all of the children, on both sides of the street, attended Mass at St. John's every Sunday. It was the difference in where the children learned to read and write that relegated the public school kids to their role as sinful pagans.

MR. FATHER

The dye was usually cast by the Catholic school kids with a catchy little war cry that had been passed down through the years.

Stinkin' Lincoln
What are they drinkin'?
Beer or wine?
Oh my gosh, it's turpentine!

The Stinkin' Lincolns had never composed a verbal comeback as eloquent and melodious as their pious adversaries. They preferred to retaliate with obscenities, fists, and rocks.

Mike and Ted Bassano were two of the Stinkin' Lincolns who participated in the weekly crusade. The brothers, separated in age by only sixteen months, relished the chance to tussle with the Catholic school kids.

Following religious education classes, Mike and Ted headed home to 23 Mill Street, a block up from St. John's. Mike, Ted, and their parents lived in the downstairs apartment of a white shingled two-family house. The upstairs apartment was occupied by their father's sister, Aunt Justine, her husband, and Mike's five cousins.

One door up from Mike's house, on the corner of Mill Street and Vestal Avenue, stood Southside Barber Shop. The establishment was owned by Mike's grandfather and run by Mike's dad (Mike Sr.) and his Uncle Carmen. The barbers buzzed and trimmed every father and son within a mile radius.

Built up on the southern bank of the Susquehanna River, the south side was predominately a mix of first and second generation Irish and Italians. Families with surnames like Stracuzzi, McCormack, Gallagher, Scarcelli, DiPaolo, and Gibbons lived next door to one another. It was a constellation of households brought together each week for Mass, choir, the Holy Name Society and the Legion of Mary.

"We were suspicious of anyone who said they went to a church with a name that didn't begin with 'Saint'," Mike recalls.

Mike's dad was a soft spoken barber who nodded and agreed as his clientele made small talk. From the time Mike and Ted could hold a broom handle, they knew what it meant to earn their keep. He and Ted were paid a dollar a week to sweep, straighten and sit—sweep the floors, straighten up magazines and comic books, and sit in the barber chairs. Throughout their youths, the boys were involuntary guinea pigs to the barbers' explorations into new hair styles and tonics. The boys stared into the mirror as the shape and length of their black locks took on new forms. When experiments went awry, their father and Uncle Carmen solved the problem by simply clipping the boys' hair down to the scalp.

Mike was shy and abided by his father's way of running things. Ted was more assertive. After a few years without a raise, Ted decided his weekly wage was not sufficient.

"Dad, I'm more than a year older than Mike," Ted said. "I think it's time I got a raise. How 'bout I get two bucks a week now?"

Mike Sr. lit up a Lucky Strike, inhaled, and blew out his answer.

"How 'bout this Teddy? You're fired."

Mike Sr. called over his younger son.

"Mikey—you've been promoted. You're gonna' do Teddy's work along with your own and get his dollar."

Mike often wandered into St. John's on his walks home from Lincoln Elementary.

"That immense structure drew me in," Mike recalls. "I used to walk into the church and think, 'Wow this place is big!'"

Mike felt drawn to the back of the church, where he would gaze up at a five-foot wooden cross with a ceramic likeness of Jesus nailed to it. Mike learned in religious education classes that, "Jesus had suffered and died for our sins." This explanation, repeated every Tuesday afternoon, didn't make sense to the little boy (and still doesn't to this day).

Mike looked up at Jesus and asked in wonderment, *"Why*

did you do this?" He sat quietly in the empty church, imagining how each nail must have felt going into Jesus' hands. He thought, "How would my mother feel if she saw me nailed to a couple pieces of wood?"

Mike was in awe of the bearded man's bravery. He didn't quite understand why anyone would voluntarily agree to such agony, but at that point in his life it didn't matter.

"I didn't know what the reason was," Mike recalls. "I just felt that if I followed this Jesus guy, I would be able to endure anything. Mickey Mantle and Jesus were my heroes."

Mike detested going to the doctor's office for physicals before the school year started, because it meant painful inoculations. He learned to get through it by closing his eyes just before the needle pierced his skin, saying to himself, "At least it's not a nail."

By the time he was nine-years-old, Mike was telling his family that he wanted to be a priest. He liked to play army and climb trees like the other boys in the neighborhood, but his favorite activity was playing priest. Holding makeshift Masses in his backyard, Mike stood on the top step of a dog kennel imitating what he witnessed every Sunday at St. John's. Cousins and neighborhood kids stood below him. He solemnly placed candy Necco Wafers on their tongues, telling them it was the "Body of Christ." He ended each Mass with an ad lib blessing and then sent his small congregation on their way.

SANTIAGO, CHILE — 1988

Mike awoke one Sunday morning in late summer and gathered his alb and lectionary for Mass. He walked out his front door, ready to make his way through the gravelly streets of La Bandera—a slum (poblacion) on the periphery of the Chilean capital. A resident of Santiago for only three months, he welcomed the daily challenges that living in squalor had presented thus far. With each new experience, preconceptions were replaced by the authentic realities of living in a new culture. Mike felt that his call to serve the poor finally coalesced with what the world needed from him. He was exactly where he wanted to be. In contrast, the dejected inhabitants of his neighborhood wanted to be anywhere but La Bandera.

Before he reached the end of his block that March day, a voice called out, "Padre, Padre."

The priest turned around to see a young man limping toward him.

"Padre, I was shot in the leg and the bullet is still in there."

Mike knelt down to get a better look at the young man's festering wound. Juan, nineteen-years-old, told Mike that two months earlier the military had raided his neighborhood searching for dissidents. Juan had regularly demonstrated against Chile's military regime, in power since 1973. He ran from the armed soldiers, fearful of imprisonment and torture. The soldiers opened fire on the teenager. Juan was handcuffed and dragged away. For two months, he was tortured. Juan was labeled a communist by his jailers—yet anyone who spoke out against the country's fascist regime, regardless of political affiliation, was branded a communist. Juan's predicament was the result of a comprehensive directive from the country's chief soldier, Generalissimo Augusto Pinochet, to squelch dissent.

Let it be said that Pinochet was not a communist. The General was, however, a fan of attaching electrodes to the genitalia of his detractors and watching them squirm. During Pinochet's seventeen year reign, tens of thousands of Chileans were jailed and tortured. Pinochet gave the orders to put hydrochloric acid into water cannons that scorched the skin of protestors demonstrating for truth. But he was not a communist, and during the Cold War this was a crucial propaganda tool necessary in convincing an uninformed American public that soulless autocrats like the Chilean dictator could be classified as an ally.

"Have you seen a doctor?" Mike asked.

Juan told Mike that his wound had been hastily sewn up

in jail. Following his release, Juan went to a hospital where the decision was made to leave the projectile in his leg and let his skin heal over it. Medical resources for the poor under Pinochet were deliberately scarce. Juan's wound was dressed and the teenager was sent back to the streets.

"Can you help me Padre?" Juan asked.

Mike had no reply. The violence that brought the teenager to him in this condition made no sense. *"This is just a kid,"* he thought.

The bloody river of injustice that had been coursing its way through Latin America for generations was now splashing in Mike's face and he didn't like it. Though warned of the villainy he would inevitably encounter, the priest felt unbridled rage for the first time in his life. Mike knew his life was about to change. No book or lecture could have prepared him for this moment. Playing the role of comforting priest for parents whose sons and daughters were being kidnapped and tortured would not be sufficient. He could not passively preach from the pulpit that heaven held a special place for the vanquished. Unless he made the choice to walk along side the poor and the oppressed as an equal, he would never truly understand their plight. Knowing his assimilation into the new culture was over, Mike said to himself, *"There's no turning back now. I'm ready."*

Mike landed in Santiago in late December of 1987, almost four years to the day he first heard the call to *"Go to Maryknoll."* He spent his first day at Maryknoll's Chilean headquarters in an upscale area of Santiago. Sitting on a veranda with some fellow missioners, Mike sipped on a gin and tonic, enjoying a luxury and security that would soon be gone.

The next day, as Mike rode the bus that would take him to his new home, buildings turned into shacks and asphalt into gravel. Mike stepped off the bus at one of the stops in La Bandera, a cascade of dilapidation. He walked a few blocks and opened the gate to what would be his house for the next two years. He was welcomed by his new housemates, Gary Winslow and Jan Barker. Gary was a Catholic priest, also on his first mission. Jan was a lay missioner. They showed him to his room, where they thought he would unpack his suitcase and settle in. Yet he threw his bag on the bed and walked back out into the living room.

"I was so excited," Mike recalls. "I couldn't wait to get out there and get right into it. I had been waiting for this moment for so long."

The body language of his housemates displayed a contentedness in staying put. It was the middle of summer in the southern hemisphere and the heat was oppressive. Mike found it odd though, that they had not planned some sort of tour of the neighborhood, allowing him to get his bearings. They told him it was their day off and that they would show him around the next day.

Mike couldn't wait another day. Four years had been long enough. He hadn't flown five thousand miles south to sit on a couch. He would have to show himself around.

"My hands shook as I closed the gate to leave the house," Mike recalls. "I said to myself, *'If I fail, then I fail.'*"

Mike walked around the neighborhood. He smiled and said hello to the men and women he passed. His Italian complexion and black hair were features not noticeably different than that of his new neighbors. After exploring the neighborhood for an hour, he turned the corner, saw some kids playing soccer, and joined in the game. During a break, one of the kids asked him who he was.

"Me llamo Padre Miguel."

"Really, you're a priest?" one child asked.

"So, where are you from?" another asked, noticing his accent.

Mike had spent the previous five months in Bolivia, studying Spanish and living with a family of Chilean exiles. Still, his grammar and accent were far from perfect.

"I'm from New York in the United States," he said.

Mike explained to the kids it was his first day in La Bandera.

"My name is Carlito," one of the children said. "Let me show you around."

Carlito took Mike's hand and led him through the neighborhood.

"Padre Miguel," Carlito said, "you don't want to walk down to that corner. That's where all the drug dealers hang out. They'll kill you. And down there is where all the prostitutes do business. After the sun goes down, you shouldn't be outside. If the gangs don't get you, the drug addicts will."

As they walked the dusty streets, Carlito pointed out where Mike could buy food and other odds and ends. Then they came upon the front of a wooden shack. It was no larger than the living room of an average American home.

"...and this is my house," Carlito said. "Come in and meet my mother."

"She offered me some bread and coffee," Mike recalls. "I learned later that Carlito's father had died. He was an alcoholic and Carlito's mother drank a lot too. She beat the boy on a regular basis."

Mike's bold little tour guide spent much of his time outside of the home as a way of avoiding confrontation with his mother.

"Carlito was the most street smart nine-year-old I'd ever met," Mike remembers. "He walked through the streets without fear. In those early days, *I* felt like a child. He taught me how to make my way through La Bandera."

During Mike's two years in La Bandera, he saw Carlito frequently. Sometimes they would run into one another on the street. During the week, Mike would stop into Carlito's house at nighttime to say hello. Then there were times when Carlito would show up at Mike's house unannounced. Ragged clothes hanging off his body, the boy would come to Mike with either a bruised face or an empty belly. Mike accommodated Carlito, whatever his needs were. He owed the boy.

The sights and sounds of Mike's new world were a lot to take in during those first days. He looked forward to saying Mass, as Liturgy would provide a familiarity to his new setting. On his first Sunday, his housemates provided him with directions, but Mike found them hard to follow.

"I thought they might take me there, but I think they thought I knew my way around better than I did. They told me after a few rights and lefts, I'd spot the chapel."

Mike headed out, but found himself lost within minutes.

"I couldn't believe it," Mike recalls. "Here I was, the new guy, and I was going to be late for my first Mass. I was just standing there in the middle of the street, completely lost."

That's when Mike met Loreto.

"Excuse me sir—would you like to buy some plums?" a

young girl asked, a bowl of ripe fruit set on a table in front of her.

Mike turned to the girl with a confused look on his face.

"Is there something wrong?"

"I think I've lost my way. Do you know where the chapel is?"

Loreto saw that Mike had a leather bound book in his hand and an alb resting on one of his forearms.

"Are you a priest?"

"Yes. I'm a priest, I'm lost, and I'm late for Mass."

Loreto immediately shared Mike's sense of urgency and came out from behind her table.

Looking up the street, she said, "You are close Padre, don't worry. If you keep walking up that way two blocks, you will see it on your right. There is a small cross above the door."

"What's your name?" Mike asked.

"Loreto Ulloa."

"Well, Loreto Ulloa, I'm Padre Miguel. Thank you for your directions."

Hustling up the street, Mike heard Loreto call out to him. He turned around and saw her running toward him.

"Padre, this is for you," she said, bowing her head and offering him one of her plums.

It was a gift he would have never received had he not been lost. Mike would return to Loreto's house the next week. In time, he grew close to the little girl and her family.

After only a few weeks in La Bandera, Mike was recognized as the Padre. The families of the neighborhood would yell for him to come in and visit as he made his rounds through the poblacion. When Mike spent time with families, he was a confidante to the adults and a playmate for the children. He would listen to parents as they spoke of unemployment, marital issues, and addiction. Their conversations often led to tears. Mike would counter the sadness the children saw in their parents' eyes by bringing along his guitar, an instrument he had taught himself to play in the seminary.

"Music was a wonderful way to connect with the kids," Mike recalls. "They would teach me new songs and that helped with my vocabulary. I would pick out the melody until I had it right. The kids always enjoyed my visits with the guitar."

When he walked into their meager homes, they would invariably offer him food.

"If I came at dinner time," Mike recalls, "they would yell into the kitchen 'Mas aqua a la sopa' (More water to the soup). I always loved that expression. They were saying 'We don't have anything, but hell, we'll share it with you."

Mike felt uncomfortable accepting anything from those who had so little.

"They always felt honored when I came to their houses. Sometimes I would look in the kitchen and they would be offering me their last piece of bread. I didn't need it, but by turning it down, I was rejecting them. I had to accept something to let them save face. I learned that by just asking for a cup of tea, I could receive their offer without offending them."

Mike realized early on that leaving the poblacion, if only for a few hours a week, was a necessity.

"I had to keep one foot in and one foot out," Mike says. "In order to serve their needs, I had to spoil myself sometimes. It was a form of self-preservation."

Wednesdays were half-price movie day at the theaters in downtown Santiago. For Mike, movies had always served as a brief escape from life's daily struggles. One Wednesday evening during his first year, Mike hopped on a bus to return home after seeing a double feature. He closed his eyes, intending to catch a few winks, but fell into a deep sleep and missed his stop.

"End of the line. You have to get off," the bus driver said, waking up the groggy priest.

Mike stepped off the bus onto a dark and empty street. Other than knowing he was somewhere in La Bandera, an area that housed over 100,000 people, he was lost. He began walking at a brisk pace, hoping he was headed in the right direction. In the pitch black of night, it was difficult to make out much of anything. From the darkness came three teenagers.

"One put a knife to my throat and the other two grabbed my arms," Mike recalls. "I had enough sense not to resist— otherwise they would have slit my throat. I just kept saying, 'I'm a priest! I'm a priest!'"

Within seconds, they pilfered Mike's wallet, grabbed his glasses, and threw him to the ground.

"I couldn't see a thing. I stood up and dusted myself off. I was certain I'd get robbed again and lucky if I made it home alive."

He thought about knocking on a door and asking for help, but decided that might not be the smartest thing to do. People in his neighborhood knew him as Padre Miguel. On this street, he was just a stranger. A rumbling engine interrupted his frantic thoughts. When he turned around, he saw two blurry lights coming toward him. It was a taxi.

"Now, no one had the guts to drive into La Bandera at night for fear of being robbed or killed." Mike recalls. "You never saw cabs after nightfall. But there it was."

"Can I give you a lift home?" The driver asked.

Blood dripping onto his collar, Mike got into the cab. He

explained that he was a priest and that he would reward the kind driver for helping him. The cab arrived at Mike's house ten minutes later. He told the driver to wait a minute while he went into his house to get some money.

"Don't bother, Padre," the driver said.

The cabbie drove off into the night as quickly as he had appeared.

"The next day, we heard that a cab driver had been killed in La Bandera the night before," Mike remembers. "I never knew if it was him. I didn't ask him what his name was because I was so flustered. He was an angel though—no doubt about it."

"They certainly weren't short," Mike says, of the two-hour-long Masses in La Bandera.

"Everyone sang their hearts out for ten or fifteen minutes," Mike remembers. "Then we would begin *Hechos de Vida* (Deeds of Life)."

Hechos de Vida was a ritual where the happenings in the poblacion were made known to one another.

"We were saying, 'How can we give thanks if we don't know what is taking place around us?'" Mike recalls.

Most of what was offered up illustrated the desperate scenarios that living in squalor involved. The Masses were small, usually fifty people or so. It wasn't uncommon for everyone to say something.

> *"My son went missing three days ago. The police threw him on a bus. I don't know where he is. Please pray for me."*

> *"I have no money. My husband left a month ago and I have three hungry mouths to feed."*

> *"I thought my situation was bad, but my children are alive and healthy. I still have my husband. He drinks all the time — but I still have him. Thank you, Lord."*

"That's when the church came alive for me," Mike remembers. "They were so observant and in tune with the intangibles. Most times, all they could offer up were kind words. That was enough to keep them going."

One rainy Sunday morning, Mike trudged into a chapel for Mass. When *Hechos De Vida* commenced, Mike noticed a man in the congregation staring at his muddy shoes. When the time came for the man to speak, he stood up and pointed to Mike.

"Look — Padre Miguel's shoes are covered in mud."

The congregation took notice. Mike was embarrassed and thought for a moment about leaving the altar to wipe them down. Then the man turned around to the congregation pro-claiming, "This is a sign you see. Padre Miguel has come to walk among us and share in our suffering."

Mike has not shined his shoes since that day.

Emerging in the late sixties and early seventies, a new religious perspective, Liberation Theology, challenged the Catholic Church to take an active stance in the lives of the poor and the oppressed. Peruvian Jesuit, Gustavo Gutierrez, and Brazilian Franciscan, Leonardo Boff, posited that Jesus had, himself, arisen from a poor background to challenge the oppression and injustice of his time. Sin to this new theology was defined as one's inhumanity to his fellow Man. As much a political movement as a theology, progressive Latin American clergy argued that God did not remain indifferent to the evils that existed in the present. Rather, the divine revealed itself through the struggle of the downtrodden. They believed that Christians on all levels could not remain apathetic to the plight of the poor or unconcerned regarding open violations of human rights.

For those Christians living under the rule of despots like Pinochet, Liberation Theology, and more importantly, the action the theology called for, gained overwhelming popularity in Latin America. Christian Base Communities (CBC's) were the grassroots manifestation of Liberation Theology, focusing on how scripture could reveal solutions to their issues. Lack of clergy in rural communities and slums, meant CBC's were often organized and directed by laypeople.

The meetings of CBC's followed a basic routine. A Gospel passage would be read. Then discussion would be opened up to the group regarding how the reading related to their specific political or socio-economic situation. Next, the group would discuss the ways in which they could address the issue in a non-violent manner (i.e. boycott, strike, protest, etc.). Lastly, the action would be organized and carried out. The grassroots dynamic of CBC's gave Scripture a living quality to the lives of the poor.

"It wasn't abstract to them," Mike recalls. "It was telling people that Jesus lives in the present."

Over the ten years Mike lived in the slums, he and other clergy were responsible for congregations spread over large areas, making it impossible for them to be present at every Mass.

"We were lucky if we could get to some parishes once a month," Mike recalls.

Still, Mike attended CBC meetings nightly. During his first months, he just listened. The difficulties parishioners faced were daunting. It was inconceivable for the new priest not to side with them. Mike had never believed that doctrinal interpretations were cut and dry. He felt those holding Vatican addresses weren't necessarily more privy to the intent of Scripture.

Heavy criticism came down from Rome as Liberation Theology grew in popularity during the seventies and eighties. The Vatican argued the theology relegated Jesus to the role of political figure, thereby diminishing his divinity. The bottom-up dynamic of CBC's conflicted with the hierarchical structure within the Church. Though the Vatican had always played a major role in the international political arena, higher-ups in Rome felt CBC's were acting without proper sanction. Church policy was discussed at councils and then protocol was implemented via downward flowing channels. The idea that the poor and uneducated had the wisdom to relate religious teachings of the past to current injustice was foreign to many in Rome. This was, in fact, how the Church had begun. However, those isolated from the realities of torture, death squads, and contempt for the poor felt that this new theology lacked the profundity of earlier revelation.

Cardinal Joseph Ratzinger, now Pope Benedict XVI, was one of many Vatican elites who formally condemned Liberation Theology and Christian Base Communities as being too Marxist in tone and practice. He felt that the Latin

American interpretation of the Gospels was more about class struggle than it was about spiritual salvation. Yet by the fall of '84, when Ratzinger publicly denounced Liberation Theology, there were already thousands of CBC's successfully challenging repressive regimes. When Mike arrived in Chile in late '87, CBC's and Liberation Theology were stubborn stains on the fabric of Latin American injustice. Vatican denunciation had little to no effect in washing them out.

Mike reveled in the enthusiasm he witnessed during CBC meetings. The parishioners he met were active and committed. The Gospels were a vehicle of hope. Enthusiasm turned solemn though, when he walked out of his house one day and met a young man with a bullet in his leg.

three

A TRIP TO THE CANDY STORE
SANTIAGO — 1988

Mike's phone rang as night fell on La Bandera.

"Miguelito, this is Chicorio."

"Chicorio—Que pasa?" Mike asked.

"We're taking the kids shopping tomorrow and I was wondering if you wanted to meet us."

"I'm not sure. What time were you thinking?"

"We'll be at the candy store around one o'clock."

"I can't. I have a meeting tomorrow afternoon. I'm sorry."

"Okay, maybe some other time."

"Adios Chicorio," Mike said, hanging up on the line he suspected was tapped by the Chilean National Information Agency (CNI).

The next day he boarded a bus bound for the center of

MR. FATHER

Santiago. Despite his answer to Chicorio the night before, he would meet up with his friend at the candy store.

His bus pulled over at a stop on Alameda Avenue. The street was crowded with lunch time pedestrians and motor traffic. The clock above a bank read 12:50 p.m. He was early. Mike walked up to the window of a men's clothing store and stared at a mannequin dressed in a suit. In the reflection of the window he spotted an acquaintance, but decided not to say hello. He walked over to a news stand and flipped through a magazine. After wiping off the lenses of his glasses, he took note of soldiers manning their posts along the thoroughfare. As he knelt down to tie his shoe laces, he looked up at the clock again. It read 1 p.m. It was time to go to the candy store.

Mike and fifty other people stepped off the curb and onto the street, halting traffic. A banner unfolded, a mast for the men and women who quickly flocked behind it. The banner read, *El Movimiento Contra Tortura* (The Movement Against Torture). The song *Yo Te Nombre Libertad* (I Name You Freedom) intoned from their mouths as they marched down the middle of the street.

> *For the flowers torn*
> *On the grass trampled*
> *For trees pruned*

For the tortured bodies
I write your name
on the walls of my city
I write your name
on the walls of my city
Your true name
Your name and other names
not named for fear
On land, overrun
For the conquered peoples
For people suppressed
Exploited by men
Of those killed in the fire
For the just executed
For the hero murdered
By the fires extinguished
I name you Freedom

As the song concluded, Mike and his fellow demonstrators continued to march forward. They recited the names of the disappeared, "Alicia Herrea, Ariel Salinas, David Silberman..."

The military was always ready to assemble as quickly as the demonstrators. Armed with machine guns and batons, soldiers geared up to squash the assemblage. A bus equipped with a water cannon pulled around the corner and took aim. Arm-in-arm, the group clenched one another tightly as the soldiers surrounded them. Then the beatings began. Mike raised his arms to his head as soldiers swung their batons indiscriminately. They fired their guns into the air in an attempt to disperse the crowd.

Many of the demonstrators were handcuffed and thrown into military buses bound for jail. Yet they were never able to apprehend everyone. On this day, Mike fled as he heard his fellow protestors cry out in pain. He and other demonstrators not arrested, met twenty minutes later in the office of a sympathizer. They made an assessment of who had been detained or if anyone needed medical assistance. Broken limbs and bloody contusions were common. The group then sent out members to the jails where the arrested were most likely held.

The military was evasive when it came to acknowledging whether or not individuals were being held in a particular facility. Sometimes demonstrators were released after a few hours. Other times it was weeks or months. If the military believed that one of their captives was a key conspirator or leader, they were tortured.

A Trip to the Candy Store

From 1988 to 1992, Mike marched in over one-hundred human rights protests like the one just described. Along with *El Movimiento Contra Tortura*, Mike joined the *Agrapacion Familieres de los Detenitos y Desaparacedo* (Family Members of the Detained and Disappeared). The *AFDD* was a group established in 1974, consisting mostly of mothers whose children had been disappeared following the Pinochet coup.

"They were the bravest women I'd ever met," Mike recalls. "They hadn't seen their children for years. They didn't even know if they were alive."

Mike's mentor during his years of protest was a young man in his late twenties named Claudio Escobar, or Chicorio (cabbage head), as he was affectionately called by his friends.

"Claudio was committed to his country," Mike recalls. "He had a sixth sense when it came to protests. He knew when to pick and choose battles — when we would stand strong and when it was time to run and march another day. In the beginning of my involvement, he saw that I couldn't tell the difference, so he kept an eye on me."

On two occasions, Claudio proved his valor to his gringo friend. During one of Mike's first protests, the priest was beaten, pushed to the asphalt, and handcuffed. Amidst the chaos, Claudio lost sight of Mike, as the priest was thrown into a military bus.

"Miguelito! Where is Miguelito?" Claudio shouted to another protestor.

"He was arrested."

The doors of the military bus slammed shut and the vehicle began driving away. Claudio ran down the middle of the street trying to catch up with the bus. When traffic slowed, Claudio jumped up and pounded on its windows.

"You assholes!" Claudio shouted at the soldiers inside the bus. "Don't you have the balls to arrest me?"

When the military ignored him, he threw rocks.

"It's kind of funny looking back on it," Mike remembers. "There was Claudio—shouting the most degrading words I'd ever heard in Spanish."

The military was perplexed as to why Claudio wanted to be on the bus. Obligated to take action, the driver slammed down on his brakes. A soldier cuffed Claudio and threw him in with the rest of the protestors.

"What are you doing?" Mike asked his friend.

"I just thought I'd keep you company, Miguelito."

When they arrived at the detention center, the arrested were grouped into one cell. After four hours, Mike's bladder was ready to burst. Two soldiers accompanied him to the bathroom.

"I stood there with soldiers on either side of me," Mike

recalls. "I had to go so bad, but I had these guys standing right next to me with machine guns. After a couple minutes, nothing came out. I had stage fright for the first time since high school."

Mike was returned to his cell. An hour later he stood in front of a desk.

"What's your name?" the jailer asked.

"Father Michael Bassano."

"Where are you from?" The man looked up, noticing Mike's accent.

"The United States."

The guard gave him a suspicious nod and waved to his counterparts to take Mike back to the cell. After seven hours, the priest was released.

"Being an American and a priest had its advantages in these situations," Mike recalls. "Locking me up indefinitely would have caused problems for them."

By the time Mike was involved in protesting, the mothers of the *AFDD* had been organized for fourteen years. Many in the group were now in their sixties and seventies. During a protest on a Friday afternoon, 77 year-old Carmen Vivanco, a woman who had five relatives disappeared by the secret police, was clubbed by a soldier, breaking her wrist. Outraged, the *AFDD* took action the next day. Gathered in the center of the Plaza de Armas, Mike, Claudio, and a hundred other protestors cried out for the prosecution of the soldier who had beaten the old woman.

"This was one of the times I was really scared," Mike recalls. "They were ready to pounce on us."

The military moved in on the group and the beatings began again. Mike and the protestors fled across the city's central plaza toward the Metropolitan Cathedral. The Cathedral was a safe haven that uniformed military knew not to enter under any circumstances. Still, they could try to stop protestors from seeking refuge. Mike dodged a soldier who swung at his knees. He felt the hands of his fellow protestors pushing him up the stairs of the Cathedral. Then he felt someone grab the collar of his shirt, pulling him in the opposite direction. It was the firm grip of a soldier. He struggled not to fall backwards, just a couple meters from the Cathedral's doors. Out of the corner of his eye, he saw a fist strike down on the soldier's arm, freeing him. Unabated, Mike stumbled into the church.

"When I looked over," Mike recalls, "I saw it was Claudio who saved me. I would've gotten a good beating and ended up in jail. But there he was again, looking out for me."

Mike's participation in the *AFDD* and *El Movimiento*

Contra Tortura wasn't popular with many of his colleagues.

"Some of the older generation thought our involvement was futile," Mike recalls. "They felt that you could overlook the injustice. They said, 'Maybe these things have to happen in order for economic progress to take place.' Our stance was that none of the progress could be justified if human rights were being violated."

In September of 1973, when Pinochet staged the coup that brought him to power, thousands of Chileans were detained and tortured in the name of stabilizing the economic downturn that had ensued under democratically elected president, Salvador Allende. During his first years in power, Pinochet exercised no restraint in crushing any real or imagined threats. The Chilean National Intelligence Directorate, headed up by General Manuel Contreras, who would later become a CIA asset, implemented Pinochet's policies of repression. Socialists, academics, journalists, and the poor in general were shipped off to concentration camps set up around the country.

The Catholic Church of Chile initially supported the new government. Pinochet had promised a movement toward democracy once economic stability was attained. The Chilean Church had been unhappy with Salvador Allende because of his socialist policies. They were fearful that religion would be marginalized or even banned, as it had been following the socialist revolutions in Europe and Asia earlier in the century. Over the next few years however, as word got out regarding innumerable accounts of torture and murder, the Chilean Church changed its position.

The U.S. Government supported the coup of '73, but in the years following, found itself embroiled in an international public relations war with human rights organizations regarding Pinochet's crimes. Under pressure from the Carter and Reagan administrations in the late seventies and early eighties, Pinochet drew down overt violations of human rights. By employing more subtle tactics, such as kidnapping and internal espionage, he created a "friendly dictator" illusion abroad. The U.S. knew that torture was still occurring, but because Pinochet implemented more discrete methods of repression, the Americans could turn a blind eye. In addition, the spread of communism in Latin America was a viable threat to U.S. corporate interests. Having a pro-American leader on the western shore of South America was tolerable to the U.S. and its allies, even if Pinochet was a tyrant.

For close to two decades, any dissenters, including clergy who lived in the slums, were labeled communists. Brazilian Bishop, Dom Hélder Câmara, who faced a similar struggle in his country, once said, "When I give food to the poor, they

48

call me a saint. When I ask why they are poor, they call me a communist."

In 1989, Mike would learn this lesson first hand. During a protest, tear gas was launched into the air, having its desired effect on the priest. Looking for relief, he staggered into a pharmacy.

"Please—can you give me something to wash my eyes out?" he asked.

"Get the hell out of here you communist pig!" the pharmacist shouted.

The human rights groups that Mike was a part of had no political affiliations. Certainly, there were those in the groups who had been active participants in socialist organizations. Yet the *AFDD* and *El Movimiento Contra Tortura* were calling for an end to human rights violations and the release of prisoners, not revolution.

To his dismay, Mike gained street credibility in the poblaciones during this period. The Chilean media, largely controlled by the regime, received anonymous phone calls regarding the location of demonstrations minutes before they began.

"One of the goals of the movement was to bring awareness to the public of what was happening," Mike's friend, Claudio Escobar says now. "We wanted people to know that illegal detainment and torture were still occurring. Many didn't believe it. We knew that our actions would be filtered by the media. We would be described as something other than what we were. But everyone knew the media was controlled by Pinochet."

Following demonstrations, footage was beamed around the country, accompanied by misinformation. Those in the slums were immune to voices of propaganda.

"Padre Miguel, I saw you on T.V. last night," neighbors and parishioners told him.

"I think they felt pride that someone in their neighborhood was standing up for them," Mike remembers. "I had a hard time with it at first. I would ask myself, 'Am I trying to prove something?' It was nice to be recognized, but I had to reign in my pride. The movement was larger than me and my reasons for doing it had to remain pure. I would tell those who saw me, 'I know you would do the same for me if you could. You need to keep your job and raise your children—but you're always there with me in spirit.'"

Years earlier, in 1980, Pinochet had ordered a "yes" or "no" national vote (plebiscite) to reform the country's 55 year-old constitution. Full of amendments that would expand the dictator's powers, the vote, if passed, would extend Pinochet's "presidency" for another eight years. Widespread reports of voter suppression were ignored by the U.S. The rigged outcome gave Pinochet breathing room to exert his new powers.

The beginning of the end for the Pinochet regime came on October 5, 1988. The Chilean Constitution that Pinochet had restructured eight years earlier demanded a vote to decide if his reign would be extended. By '88, the U.S. felt Pinochet's policies of repression were fomenting instability rather than containing it. The U.S. government and The Vatican strongly urged Pinochet to allow equal media time for opposition groups. The U.S. State Department funded voter registration drives through its foreign assistance branch, USAID.

Still, Pinochet wielded his power over those he felt most threatened by — the poor.

"In the months before the plebiscite," Mike recalls, "plainclothed men began showing up in the poblaciones. They made all sorts of promises and bribed people into voting "yes" for Pinochet. There were rallies all over Santiago. Then the military came in buses, shooting and beating people. Two of our parishioners were killed. I was running home one night, when a neighbor grabbed me and hid me in the back of her house. I heard gunshots and people being beaten. When we heard the buses pull away, I came out and saw that they had beaten my two housemates. They broke Jan's knees."

MR. FATHER

On October 4, 1988, the night before the plebiscite, Pinochet turned off the electricity in the poblaciones.

"We didn't know what was going to happen," Mike remembers. "An autogolpe (where Pinochet would declare a state of emergency and dissolve the plebiscite) was a real threat. We sat in the dark, listening to our transistor radio. During the night we didn't hear any gunfire and there were no reports of violence."

Pinochet may have intended on continuing the violence in the poblaciones or staging an autogolpe, but the night before the plebiscite, he got a call from the U.S. State Department. They warned him, in no uncertain terms, not to poison the voting in any way. Chileans went to the polls the next day.

"It was so quiet," Mike recalls, "People stood in line patiently. At some of the polls we saw international observers making sure there wasn't any monkey business. I was amazed at how transparent the counting was. They counted the ballots right in front of us. After every "no" vote was announced, we would cheer. After a "yes" vote, there were boo's. People looked around at one another saying, 'It wasn't me.'"

The results came in the next day and Pinochet lost by ten percentage points. He agreed to relinquish political power, but national elections for a new leader wouldn't take place for another year. According to the Pinochet-amended constitution, the dictator would remain the head of the army, a post he manned until 1998. In addition, the constitution allowed him to serve as a "Senator for life" in the Chilean congress. Both were positions Pinochet used to exercise influence when calls for his prosecution arose in the years following his regime's demise. Still in control of the army, Pinochet continued to violently suppress demonstrations calling for truth.

"He did everything he could to silence us," Mike recalls. "We continued to protest."

Pinochet had done his best to cover up the violent and repressive policies his junta had carried out, but evidence was dug up all over Chile after his downfall.

"The *AFDD* and other organizations got calls from around the country saying they knew where the bodies were buried," Mike recalls. "I officiated dozens of group funerals. Most times, the families only had body parts. There was a sense of closure. The mothers could finally put their children to rest."

The tears that ran down the faces of the elderly women reminded Mike that long before he was a priest, he was a son. Their resilience was living proof that neither tyranny nor fear could expunge the maternal instinct to protect.

four

DIAMONDS ON A CHALICE
BINGHAMTON, NEW YORK via SICILY — 1930-1975

As a boy, Mike looked up to the parish priests at St. John's. He didn't completely understand the Latin Liturgy that Monsignor Robert Driscoll and Father Dennis Hartnett spoke and chanted during Mass. However, their reverence gave him the impression they were fluent in a secret vernacular, one crucial in communicating with God. The confidence they exuded was a characteristic Mike strived to personify throughout his youth.

Spiritually though, there was only one person whose belief in the unseen prevailed over piety. His mother was the template from which he would model his life of service. Fittingly, her name was Mary.

Mary Sariti-Bassano sat in the same pew at St. John's from

the time she was an adolescent until her death. She always attended Mass alone. Her boys went to Mass separately and her husband only went to church on the holidays. Sunday mornings were Mary's time. The church was as much a shelter of solace as it was a house of worship. Her pew was where the theater of past events and future challenges played out in her mind. Surrounded by a warm silence before Mass commenced, she reconciled the hardships she had faced in her life. Eyes closed and head bowed, Mary gained the strength to maintain the spiritual fortitude required to deal health problems that had plagued her since childhood. Her attendance at Mass was not born out of obligation. Mary was drawn to St. John's because, like the love of her sons, she could not live without it.

In 1930, nine-year-old Mary and her mother, Teresa, boarded the steerage section of a ship bound for New York from Messina, Sicily. Mother and child arrived at Ellis Island three weeks later. Before their sea legs left them, they were on a train to Binghamton, New York.

Mary's father, Giuseppe Sariti, was a shoe cobbler who had arrived in the States a year earlier. He, like millions of immigrants, had learned only a handful of words in English. Those who were seeking a life outside the tenements of

New York, Philadelphia and Boston, learned one invaluable phrase taught to them by family and friends that had preceded them—*Which Way E.J.?*

Endicott Johnson was one of the biggest shoe manufacturers in the U.S. The company supplied nearly every boot to the U.S. Army during World Wars I and II. George F. Johnson, the company's president, was a progressive executive whose commitment to his workers was unheard of then, and today. Johnson built and financed homes for his workers at reasonable rates. He gave his employees free healthcare, which they accessed within the company's manufacturing plants. Throughout the Great Depression, as the big cities of the east coast spiraled into economic chaos, the residents of the Triple Cities (Binghamton, Johnson City, and Endicott) remained relatively unaffected. While immigrant populations of the eastern seaboard were standing in soup lines, men like Giuseppe Sariti were lining up to punch their time cards.

Young Mary Sariti was oblivious to any of this. She just wanted to be with her mother and father. She was a scared little girl who had spells of breathlessness and fatigue. Her appendages would intermittently turn blue, the result of a bout with rheumatic fever years earlier in Sicily. The damage the bacterial infection had on the valves of her heart was permanent and symptoms slowly worsened as she grew older.

After arriving in Binghamton, Mary's family rented an apartment on the corner of Tompkins Street and Conklin Avenue, on the city's south side. A grocery store occupied the first floor of their building. Mary and her parents lived on the third floor. The elderly owners of the building, the Tierno's, lived on the second floor. The Tierno's had a granddaughter, Gloria, who was the same age as Mary. The two little girls had difficulty communicating at first, as Mary didn't speak English. Nevertheless, youthful curiosity in one another and the desire for friendship soon surpassed their language barrier.

"We didn't understand each other at first," Gloria Tierno-Salamida recalls, "so we would sing songs. Mary's dad would get out his mandolin and we sang and danced and became the best of friends. We loved singing to each other. She was the sweetest little girl."

Mary was placed in a first grade class at Benjamin Franklin School because of her language limitations. A sharp girl, she caught up to kids her own age and in no time lost her accent.

Transition into her new world was eased when she befriended another little girl who had also moved to Binghamton from out of town. Neither Justine Bassano nor Mary Sariti had any sisters, so *de facto* sisters they became.

"We were joined at the hip as kids," Justine

Bassano-Calabrisi remembers. "Anywhere my family went, Mary came with us."

While Mary was settling into life in America, her mother's adjustment to the new culture proved difficult. Teresa rarely left her apartment on Tompkins Street or the house she and Giuseppe eventually purchased a few blocks away on Evans Street. She had long periods of what was then referred to as melancholy. She had suffered from depression throughout her life, but following the births of Mary's younger, American-born brothers (Joe, Sam and Larry), her condition intensified. Her depression contributed to her isolation and vice versa. Teresa had a psychiatric breakdown when Mary was in her mid-teens and was periodically institutionalized for the remainder of her life.

The word "teenager" was not yet part of the American lexicon in the thirties. The notion that teen-years were a period of gleeful irresponsibility would come in the years following World War II. Graduating from high school was uncommon for kids in most immigrant families. So when Mary left school at fifteen, she was not an exception to the rule. The reason she left however, was not talked about in those days, as people only spoke of mental illness in uninformed whispers. Mary had no choice but to fill the hole her mother's absence left. Her lifelong role as caretaker for the boys and men in her life began.

Mary was fortunate as a teen to have a mentor living down the street. A middle-aged woman named Bambina listened to Mary despair and dream. Bambina taught Mary how to cook an array of Italian dishes. She also encouraged Mary to do the one thing that always made the young girl happy — sing.

Whenever Mary was cleaning and cooking, she brightened up the moment by singing to her little brothers. One summer, in the late thirties, Mary heard there was a talent show being held at Ross Park Amphitheater. She signed up and dragged her best friend, Justine Bassano, along for moral support.

"She sang a little opera," Justine remembers. "She didn't win nothin' — but she had a good time losin'.'"

In the periphery of Mary's teen years, was Justine's shy older brother, Michael (Mike's father).

"He had a crush on Mary since they were kids," Justine remembers. "Before the war, they dated off and on — nothin' serious."

During World War II, Mike Sr. was a soldier in Patton's army and fought in the Battle of the Bulge. He returned to Binghamton in late 1945. He courted Mary for a short time and then asked for her hand in marriage.

"When he got home that night, I asked him how it went,"

Justine recalls. "He was quiet, ya' know. He just said, 'Yeah, we're gonna' get married.' And then he walked upstairs like it was nothing.'"

By Christmas of 1948, Mike Sr. and Mary had two baby boys, Ted and Mike.

On November 19, 1959, Charlton Heston walked into Lowes State Theater in Times Square for the world premiere of *Ben Hur*. A week later, ten-year-old Mike Bassano walked into the Strand Theater in downtown Binghamton, unaware that the next four hours would lead him further into a life akin to his hero.

"I went to see the movie on a Friday night," Mike remembers. "I was enthralled. I came home and wept. I went back the next night and cried again."

The film's sprawling cinematography and its legendary chariot race drew record crowds. It was the undertone of the movie though, that affected Mike more than the action sequences or fight scenes.

"You never see Jesus' face in the movie," Mike remembers. "You only see how the simple act of giving a thirsty man water could affect the whole world. That idea made sense to me — to be of service to others in that way. I was sure that the priesthood would allow me to live that life."

Shortly after seeing the film, Mike walked down to St. John's Rectory. Monsignor Driscoll answered the door.

"Yes Michael, what can I do for you?" The gruff clergyman asked.

"You see Monsignor...I really like what you and Father Hartnett do. And well...I want to be like you. I want to be a priest."

"Sorry Michael, you'd never make it."

Before Mike could give all the reasons he thought he would be perfect for the job, Driscoll shut the door in his face. Mike was devastated. He went home feeling inadequate. For weeks, he silently anguished over the priest's glib response. He was certain his call to serve was real. Mike was forced to pit what he knew to be true of himself against what others thought of him. The event marked the first time Mike would learn to trust and nurture his inner-voice.

"I became more determined than ever that this was my path and nothing would stop me, no matter what anyone said."

Still a public school student, Mike was a dedicated altar boy into his early adolescence. He spent Sunday mornings donning a cassock and surplice, certain that one day he would be consecrating the host and wine. When he was fourteen,

Monsignor Driscoll approached him in the sacristy.

"They're consolidating St. Patrick's and St. Paul's High Schools and opening up a new one on the west side," Driscoll said. "It's only a hundred and fifty bucks a year. If you still want to be a priest, you should consider going there."

Mike was confused. *Why was the man who told him he wasn't good enough a few years earlier, now suggesting he follow a path toward priesthood?* Mike went home and told his parents about Driscoll's suggestion. Mike Sr. and Mary agreed to pay the tuition, but didn't share their son's enthusiasm.

His parents thought the priesthood would take him away from them. His mother hoped that Mike would marry a nice Italian girl, have children, and live close to home. She held priests in high regard, but her husband told her of a loneliness he saw in clergymen's eyes when he cut their hair.

Mike would learn later in life that before he had told Driscoll he wanted to become a priest, his mother had made it known to the clergyman of *her* wishes for her son.

"She went down to the rectory too," Mike's Aunt Justine remembers. "Mike was always talking about being a priest from the time he was a little kid and she didn't like it. She told the Monsignor, 'Don't encourage my son to be a priest.'"

After a few years, Driscoll could see that Mike's reverence during Mass was a sign the boy hadn't given up on his

MR. FATHER

dream. Apparently, Driscoll hoped Mike's mother had softened a bit when he suggested Mike attend Catholic school.

Mike was a standout in high school. In his senior year, he was elected class president. Printed under his picture in the 1967 Catholic Central Yearbook were his classmates' impressions of him: "unexpected vivacity...number one man in the class... sincerity and wisdom beyond his years...eager to please."

Despite his attraction to the opposite sex, the priesthood remained in the forefront of Mike's mind. As graduation approached, he let it be known to his parents he planned to enroll at Wadham's Hall the next fall. *The Hall*, in Ogdensburg, New York, was the institution where central New York's future priests began the undergraduate program that eventually led to St. Bernard's Seminary outside Rochester. Again, his parents' reaction was subdued. They never discouraged him, but appeared unenthusiastic whenever he spoke of the priesthood.

Aunt Justine remembers, "They kept saying to me, 'He won't live a normal life.'"

Mike's parents didn't want to confront him about their misgivings. Instead, they asked Mike's Uncle Carmen to investigate the depth of their son's aspirations. The family joker, they thought Carmen's carefree manner might enlighten Mike about the downsides of being a priest.

64

On a spring evening in 1967, Mike sat down in his uncle's barber chair. Carmen gave Mike a trim as the two bantered about the Yankees for a bit. Then Carmen broached the subject in a lighthearted way.

"So Mikey—you wanna' be a priest?"

"Yeah, Uncle Carm, I've wanted to be one since I was a kid."

"Well, you know what that means Mikey."

"What's that?"

"It means you can't have your own family."

"Yeah I know, but the church will be my family."

"No Mikey—you see, you won't be able to *have* a family."

Mike knew what his uncle was insinuating, but figured he'd play dumb and watch Carmen fidget a little.

"Yeah, well, I'll always have you as my family, right?" Mike said.

"Mikey—I'm talkin' about girls!"

"Ohhhh…girls, yes, yes. What about them?"

"Mikey, I hope that your father…"

Carmen looked at his nephew's reflection in the mirror. Mike put his head down and burst into laughter. Carmen, the consummate joker, realized he was being had.

"You little son of a…"

"I'm seventeen Uncle Carm. I know a thing or two."

After Mike explained his calling to serve, Carmen was

convinced Mike was on the right path. His parents weren't as easily persuaded. Mike was not oblivious to his parents' ambivalence. He sensed disapproval in their silence. He was determined though, and for the time being, he didn't let it get to him.

Mike maintained a "B" average while studying the theology and philosophy based curriculum at Wadham's Hall and St. Bernard's. As in high school, he was admired by fellow classmates and elected to the post of Student Liturgical Director ("Pope" as it was unofficially called). Although he was never going to be at the top of his class, the title and duties of being "Pope" gave him confidence. Standing next to the Bishop and the Rector during ceremonies and celebrations, he felt validated. However, as ordination grew near, he still didn't feel his parents acknowledged his dedication and commitment.

He knew communication with his father would always be awkward. Mike Sr. had difficulty expressing his emotions with anyone. That was the case with most men of that era. Still, he questioned his mother's indifference. Mike considered her to be the most spiritual person he'd ever known. He decided to write her a long letter stating exactly how he felt.

"I was pretty harsh with her, but I needed to know, 'Why haven't you supported me?' I was surprised at how candid I was with her. I had been holding it in for so long."

A few weeks later, he received his mother's response.

"She said she always wanted what was best for me. She wasn't sure that I would live a full and happy life as a priest, but now she could see that my dedication was real. I think she was afraid she wouldn't be able to protect me. Later, I explained to her that her example would always guide me. After that, she became my most vocal supporter."

Mike asked his mother if she would take charge of his ordination celebration. Mary asked Rita Sariti (her sister-in-law), Teri Chapman (her niece), and friend Dorothy Belcher to help with the plans.

"It was like putting on a wedding," Mike's cousin Teri remembers. "We sat at Aunt Mary's kitchen table going through all the details. She was so excited and wanted it to be perfect."

One night, in late January 1975, Mike put his head down to go to sleep at St. Bernard's Seminary.

"I had a dream that I was sitting in class. The door opened and the Rector of the seminary walked in. In those days, the Rector only interrupted class for two reasons. The first was that you hadn't made the cut. They sent you on your way—right then and there. The other reason was that there was a family crisis. I dreamt the Rector walked up to me and told me my mother was sick."

The next morning, Mike went about his normal routine. Sitting in class, a knock disrupted one of his lessons. It was the Rector. He called Mike out into the hallway.

"It's your mother, Mike. She's had a heart attack and she's in a coma. You need to get home."

In December of 1974, Mary Bassano made an appointment with her general practitioner, Dr. Fitzgerald. She was having bouts of breathlessness and her appendages were tingling from a lack of blood flow. Her mitro-valve was leaking. Fitzgerald told her she would die without surgery. She had undergone an open-heart operation in 1959, knowing she would eventually have to be re-opened, as the initial surgery wasn't a permanent fix. Despite advances in surgical techniques and shortened recovery time, Mary was afraid that she might die on the operating table before she saw Mike ordained. Fitzgerald begged her to have the surgery immediately. She would hear none of it.

"After Mike's ordination in May," she told friends and family. She scheduled the surgery for July of the next year.

During the last week of January 1975, Mike Sr. and his youngest son, Paul, born ten years after Mike, battled the winter flu. Paul lay on the couch between trips to the bathroom.

Mike Sr., never one to take a day off, pushed through despite having a fever. Later that week, Mary woke Mike Sr. up in the middle of the night, telling him she was coming down with what he and Paul had caught. Rather than the previous night's dinner though, Mary began throwing up blood.

Mike Sr. drove Mary up the street to Binghamton General Hospital. He parked the car in front of the emergency room door and carried his wife to a bed. The nursing staff began a workup.

"I'll be right back Mary," he told his wife. "I gotta' get the car outta' the way."

Mary went into cardiac arrest moments after her husband left the room. The nurses brought her back, but she was comatose and kept alive with a ventilator. The family held out hope for ten days. Medical staff was skeptical whether Mary would ever regain consciousness. Mike, his dad, and his brothers took shifts by her bedside.

"I wept like a little kid," Mike recalls. "My aunts and uncles told me to stop because I was upsetting my father. I didn't care at that point. I was distraught."

Hope turned irrational when Dr. Fitzgerald brought up the subject of taking his mother off the ventilator and letting her go. The doctor gave the family the night to think about it. Mike Sr. was overwhelmed by the suggestion, so Mike, his brothers, and his cousin Teri went back to Mill Street to deliberate.

After dinner, the phone rang and Mike picked it up.

"Yes, okay. Thank you Doctor Fitzgerald."

Mike's eyes welled up.

"What did he say?" Ted asked.

"He said she died a few minutes ago," Mike answered and began sobbing.

Looking back, Mike recalls, "I felt like my mother gave us the gift of not having to make the decision. When we got to the hospital, she looked at peace. She was wrapped in white sheets. She looked so serene. She knew what it was to suffer — to be hungry, to feel alone and take a long journey, not knowing the outcome. "

Throughout the ordeal, Mike's fellow seminarians and professors came down from St. Bernard's. They offered words of encouragement and listened as Mike searched for meaning. Yet it would be a phrase that his mother lived by that comforted him the most.

"Her mantra was, 'God works in mysterious ways.' From the time I was a little kid, all of life's troubles were met with these words. Her death made no sense to me, the timing especially. But I just kept reminding myself of that saying. I think that's what got me through it. She got me through it."

In the days after his mother's funeral, talk of Mike's ordination celebration, just a few months away, came up. His father told him there was no way there would be any sort of party. Feet still cemented in the old country way of mourning a spouse, his father felt celebrating anything would be disrespectful to the memory of his wife. Also in the Italian tradition, Mike Sr. thought Mike should come home indefinitely to take on the role of dutiful son.

"I had committed six years to this and now he wanted me to give it all up," Mike remembers. "As a kid, I had always gone along with the traditions I never agreed with. I knew my mother would have wanted me to finish and have a celebration. I had to put my foot down and say, 'No, I'm going back.'"

Mike felt his ordination should be as much about honoring his mother as it was about recognizing his years of hard work. Before returning to St. Bernard's, the plans for his celebration were still up in the air. His mother had been the driving force behind them.

"A quiet voice inside me said, *'Put this into the hands of Rita, Dorothy and Teri.'* They had been planning it with my mother all along. I wasn't sure my father would come around, but I couldn't worry about that anymore. It was a lesson in surrendering up control and trusting that things would work out — faith."

After a month or so, his father did come around. Mike's first Mass took place on May 18, 1975 at St. John's. He finished his sermon by proclaiming, "Joy is not the absence of suffering, but rather, the presence of God."

After consecrating the host, Mike began the second part of the ritual.

"He gave the cup to his disciples and said, take this, all of you and drink from it, this is the cup of my blood, the blood of the new and everlasting covenant. It shall be shed for you and for all, so that sins may be forgiven."

To his left, hung the crucifix that had been so instrumental in leading him toward a life of service. To his right, was the pew his mother sat in every Sunday without fail. Mike lifted his wooden chalice and said, *"Do this in memory of me."* Embossed in the chalice were three diamonds. They were the stones from his mother's engagement ring. As he looked out over the congregation, vessel raised into the air, Mike concluded his first acts *En Persona Christi*—holding his mother in his hands.

five

MATTHEW IN THE STREETS
SANTIAGO – 1991

For close to two decades, impoverished Chileans were starved of any substantive art or creative expression. As the Pinochet era came to a close, new buds of creativity began to bloom. In 1991, Mike heard that the Italian Government was sponsoring a "popular theater" course at the University of Chile. The program was designed specifically for young adults living in the poblaciones. The aim of the program was to give its participants the tools to go back into their neighborhoods and develop popular theater troupes of their own.

Popular theater is an art form that is both improvisational and interactive. By drawing an audience into a production, the intensity of a performance is heightened. A loose script is followed, but the chosen theme and the morphing of spectators into performers are what make each performance unique and engaging. Troupe members steer volunteers from the audience in a plot direction, never knowing exactly what the volunteers will bring to the piece. The uncertain environment often leads to laughter, and forces the performers to work with what they are given. When done well, the theme of the performance resonates deeply with the audience members, as they have not just observed. Popular theater is best summed up by the words of Benjamin Franklin, "Tell me and I forget. Teach me and I remember. Involve me and I learn."

Although the program was designed for young adults, Mike applied anyway. He was confident he had something to offer. From his sophomore year in high school through his years in the seminary, singing and acting provided Mike with a sense of exhilaration absent in other activities he'd tested out.

"I ran track one year," Mike recalls, "but I never really got the whole concept of training and beating the other guy. I thought, 'Why don't we just show up at the meet to see who's the fastest? Enough of this practice silliness.' The fact that I was extremely lazy didn't help matters."

Mike's mother had passed down her love of music to him.

"There was always music in my house as a kid," Mike recalls. "Either my mom was singing or Dean Martin was crooning from the record player. I loved listening and singing along, but I was shy. I stood in the back of the chorus my first year in theater at Catholic Central."

Mike watched the older kids perform and began to see himself playing a bigger part. The high school's music director was a man named Donn Sullivan. A dedicated educator, Sullivan would serve as Mike's mentor.

"Most of the men in my life were reserved," Mike recalls. "Donn kept encouraging me to come out of my shell and improve. He had a real gift. Donn taught me that music could bring people together for a common cause. It wasn't just about me and my insecurities. It was an encouraging environment and my friends pushed me to take risks."

Sullivan walked into glee club in the beginning of Mike's junior year and told the kids he wanted to put on an Operetta. The students groaned.

"*Opera? That's not hip!*" Mike remembers thinking.

Once Sullivan began teaching the songs from *Gilbert and Sullivan's Mikado*, the near century old humor and melodies grew on his amateur thespians. Mike landed the lead comedic role of *Coco*. In his senior year, he was cast in another leading role as *Sir Joseph Porter* in *HMS Pinafore*.

The positive recognition he received from his peers and audiences nurtured a confidence Mike felt lacking during his childhood. As a young priest, he directed youth groups in renditions of *Little Mary Sunshine* and *Jesus Christ Superstar*. During his first years in Chile, Mike had been playing guitar for the children of the poblaciones, but this paled in comparison to the elation of acting and directing.

"I had never been a part of popular theater," Mike says. "I wasn't a kid anymore either."

"You're a foreigner," the popular theater program's director said when Mike showed up for an initial interview. "This is meant for kids from the slums."

Mike explained that he had been living the realities of the poor for the last three years. The director told him there were a limited number of slots in the program.

"I want to be part of this," Mike said to the director, "but if it means that someone else will lose out, then I'll withdraw my application."

A few weeks later, the director called Mike and told him that an extra spot was opened up for the 43 year-old priest.

"I walked into class the first day and the kids looked at me like, *'Who's this old guy?'*" Mike recalls.

The effects of domestic abuse, drug addiction, and violence were burdens the youth of the poblaciones had carried since birth. The designers of the course felt it was paramount that the kids feel the healing power of artistic expression. The students had to creatively work through their own issues in order to lead others in their communities.

"The first day, we were asked to give a two-minute pantomime of an experience we had either witnessed or were part of during the regime," Mike recalls. "I got up and acted out what I had experienced during the protests. One young man got up right after me. He had been tortured and relived being electrocuted and beaten to a pulp. People knew what happened in the jails, but this kid showed us exactly what it was like. When he was done, he lifted up his shirt and showed us his scars. After that, we knew this was more than just an acting class."

After eight months of intensive training, the group was sent on their way to form troupes of their own. Organizing popular theater groups became part of Mike's ministry for the next six years. He worked with themes related to drug abuse, crime, and self-esteem. Still on loan to Maryknoll from the Syracuse Diocese, Mike convinced Bishop Joseph O'Keefe to extend his leave for another five years in 1992.

Once a month, Mike took an hour-long bus ride from Santiago to Rancagua, the home of the Santa Maria de Miraflores Monastery. Mike had been taught in the seminary to always seek out spiritual guidance from fellow clergy.

Walking the grounds of the trappist monastery, Mike shared his personal and professional yearnings with Padre Adriano Rojas. Adriano had been recommended as a reliable source of spiritual insight to Mike by his colleagues.

"The solitude of the monastery allowed me to get away from the volume of the city," Mike recalls. "Adriano and I spoke of how my life was unfolding. Monks are great listeners."

In September 1993, Mike's conversations with Adriano revolved around how Mike might coalesce what he had learned throughout his life into a unifying venture.

"Have you ever thought of dramatizing the Gospels in the streets?" Adriano asked Mike.

"You mean with the kids?"

"No, just you—in the central plaza of Santiago."

"I don't think so," Mike said, intimidated.

"Why not?"

"I don't like preaching to people. I've seen the fundamentalists down there on their soap boxes and no one listens. All that repent stuff just isn't me."

"I didn't say preach," Rojas replied. "I said dramatize. You'd just be sharing a story—one that every single person in this country is familiar with. Invite the people to be a part of it. You know how to do that."

"Which Gospel? Where would I begin?"

"I don't know, Mike, but your resistance to the idea tells me there might be something to this."

On the bus ride back home to Santiago that evening, Mike couldn't stop thinking about Adriano's suggestion. He stared at the ceiling that night, trying to envision how he might pull it off. Over the next weeks, he flipped through *Matthew, Mark, Luke* and *John.*

"I had memorized verses before," Mike remembers thinking, "but an entire Gospel? No way. It was just too much."

A month later, Mike was at a get together with some fellow popular theater directors when he saw his friend, Juan Cuevas. Cuevas had dramatized *Romeo and Juliet* in the streets of Santiago and his wife, Maria Cánepa, was a professional actress. Mike told Juan that he had been thinking about a one-man project, but was discouraged because he didn't know where to begin.

"I'll just stick to directing for now," he told Juan.

"But Miguel, Maria did a one act play based on the *Gospel of Matthew* a few years back."

"She did?" Mike asked, his eyes bulging out of their sockets. "Do you still have the script?"

"Of course I do."

Cuevas sent Mike the script. He was not bothered that

it was twenty pages of formal Spanish and not written in a popular theater format.

"It was a gift from God," Mike says. "Adriano told me to be patient, but I was doubtful. When I looked at the script, I knew I could work with it."

Mike dedicated the month of December 1993 to revising the script. He changed the formal Spanish to common vernacular. He had Juan and other friends look at his revisions and based on their feedback made more changes. By New Year's Day 1994, exactly ten years to the day that he had heard the call to serve abroad, the script was ready. He gave himself twenty days to memorize it.

While rehearsing his lines one evening, Mike realized that props were needed. A chair was necessary for the *Sermon on the Mount*, as Jesus was sitting when he shared *The Beatitudes*. For the parable of *The Sower*, he needed a basket. These items could be procured easily enough. Yet for the *Crucifixion* scene, he would need a wooden cross built approximate to his height.

"I'm not the least bit handy," Mike says.

Mike was now living in the poblacion of Huamachuco. A few months earlier, he had run into a scruffy looking adolescent huffing glue behind a chapel.

"Buenos Dias, Padre," Manolo said, his eyes glazed over.

Mike sat down to talk with Manolo and listened as the

young boy told him about his life. Manolo lived with his grandmother and his five brothers in a shack the size of a one-car garage. By the time he hit puberty, Manolo had made a name for himself as a clever thief. Whenever mischief occurred in the neighborhood, Manolo was a suspect. After a man was killed during a robbery, the police went looking for Manolo. He spent three days in a jail cell being beaten and electrocuted. He was innocent of the crime and released when no useful information was elicited. The experience perpetuated Manolo's self-image as a degenerate.

"He was a good kid who had nothing," Mike recalls. "He was on his own from day one."

After their first meeting, Mike visited with Manolo and his family on a weekly basis.

"I don't know what I'm gonna' do with him Padre," Manolo's grandmother told Mike one afternoon.

"Tell me, Manolo, what do you like to do?" Mike asked.

"I like to build things, Padre."

Months later, when Mike needed a cross built, he went to Manolo's house and hired him. Mike purchased some lumber and told Manolo he wanted a wooden cross with a sturdy platform. Manolo showed up at Mike's house a few days later with a cross, precise to Mike's specifications. It was exactly what they both needed.

"I paid him for his work," Mike recalls, "but the pride on his face told me that the money didn't matter. He had done something he could be proud of."

"So you're taking this into the city?" Manolo asked Mike.

"I'm going next Thursday. Do you want to come along? I could use some help."

"No way, Padre Miguel. You're braver than me."

On Thursday, January 20, 1994, Mike was awoken by butterflies fluttering in his stomach. He looked over his script. *I must be nuts*, he thought. By 11 a.m., he was dressed in a white alb, lugging his props to the bus stop. He sat for a couple minutes with his cross, chair, basket, and guitar. As the bus pulled up, he hobbled toward the vehicle's folding doors. The driver took one look at him, closed the doors, and drove away. Dust billowing around him, his discouragement was short-lived. Mike had an ally on the bus.

"That's Padre Miguel!" an elderly woman yelled at the bus driver. "Pull this bus over right now! He's a priest."

The bus halted half a block away and the woman waved out a window, beckoning Mike to hurry along. Gasping for air, he hauled his props onto the bus and took a seat. When he gathered himself, he looked around to see suspicious eyes staring at him. He smiled, but the passengers quickly looked away.

"I must have looked like a lunatic," Mike recalls.

A block away from the Plaza de Armas, Mike carried his props off the bus.

"I was scared shitless," he remembers.

Only a few years earlier, Mike had made countless trips into the city, knowing that during the protests there was a good chance he would be beaten and arrested. On this day, he was just as fearful. He walked past evangelicals shouting about *The End of Days* and *Eternal Damnation*. In an open area, in front of the Metropolitan Cathedral, he set down his gear, strummed a couple chords on his guitar and began playing *Ode to Joy*. A few dozen people gathered around, some singing along with him.

"Chileans were very curious after the regime," Mike recalls. "They were interested in any form of free expression. I played a few songs and that drew people in."

After he got the attention of lunchtime pedestrians, he began the story. He started with the birth of Jesus by snatching a woman from the crowd.

"This is Mary," Mike said with his arm around her.

"Now, Mary was pregnant with the child of the Holy Spirit."

Mike then grabbed a middle-aged man from the audience, saying, *"But her husband Joseph was just a man and did not want to put her to shame. Then the angel of the Lord came to*

Joseph in a dream. 'Do not fear to take Mary as your wife, for she is pregnant with the child of the Holy Spirit. You will have a son and you will name him Jesus."

Mike asked the man, "You're going to name him Jesus, right? You're not going to name him Paco or Ricardo, are you?"

The audience broke out in laughter.

"Then Herod summoned the Three Wise Men," Mike said looking out into the crowd. He pointed to three young men and called them over.

"Now these guys look pretty wise to me. Are you wise?" Mike asked them.

"I am," one of them replied, "but my friends here…I'm not sure."

Following the *Nativity* scene, Mike moved on to the *Sermon on the Mount*. He pulled up his chair and asked the crowd to move in closer.

"I wanted it to be an intimate setting. When they gathered around me, I was able to look each of them in the eyes and share *The Beatitudes*."

> *Blessed are the poor in spirit, for theirs is the kingdom of heaven.*

> *Blessed are those who mourn, for they shall be comforted.*

> *Blessed are the gentle, for they shall inherit the earth.*

Blessed are those who hunger and thirst for righteousness, for they shall be satisfied.

Blessed are the merciful, for they shall receive mercy.

Blessed are the pure in heart, for they shall see God.

Blessed are the peacemakers, for they shall be called sons of God.

Blessed are those who have been persecuted for the sake of righteousness, for theirs is the kingdom of heaven.

Blessed are you when people insult you and persecute you, and falsely say all kinds of evil against you because of Me.

Rejoice and be glad, for your reward in heaven is great; for in the same way they persecuted the prophets who were before you.

The *Gospel of Matthew* had originally been written to attract followers of Judaism into what was simply known as *The Way* during the early centuries of Christianity. Compared to the other three Gospels, *Matthew* has a paternalistic tone, similar to the *Old Testament*. However, themes of social justice, as seen in *The Beatitudes*, are undeniably present in *Matthew*. For a nation just beginning to heal from its own persecution, it fit perfectly with Mike's performance. He connected with the crowd in a way he may not have been able to, had his script been based on *Mark, Luke* or *John.*

"I could see in their eyes that they understood its relevance," Mike recalls.

He recounted the parable of *The Sower.* As he spoke, a woman walked within the perimeter of the crowd with the wicker basket, pretending to toss seeds to the ground.

> *"Don't you understand this parable?" Jesus said. "The farmer sows the word. Some people are like seed along the path, where the word is sown. As soon as they hear it, evil comes and takes away the word that was sown in them. Others, like seed sown on rocky places, hear the word and at once receive it with joy. But since they have no root, they last only a short time. When trouble or persecution comes because of the word, they quickly fall away. Still others, like seed sown among thorns, hear the word; but the worries of this life, the deceitfulness of wealth and the desires for other things come in and choke the word, making it unfruitful. Others, like seed sown on good soil, hear the word, accept it, and produce a crop — thirty, sixty or even a hundred times what was sown."*

The crowd grew as Mike began *Chapter 25* of *Matthew,* where the message of personal responsibility and justice merge.

> *"When the Son of Man comes in his glory, and*

*all the angels with him, he will sit on his throne
in heavenly glory. All the nations will be gathered
before him, and he will separate the people, one from
another, as a shepherd separates the sheep from the
goats. He will put the sheep on his right and the
goats on his left."*

Mike then separated his audience into two groups.

"Alright, those of you on the right are the sheep," Mike
said. "Let me hear a loud 'baaaah.'"

Only a few people went along at first.

"Come on, I can't hear you," he yelled over their heads.

"Baaaah," the sheep yelled, looking at one another and
giggling.

He walked over to the other group.

"You're the goats!" Mike said in a disparaging tone. "Let
me hear you 'bleeet'."

The goats responded with a hearty chorus of "bleeets."

Goats and sheep in place, Mike continued.

*Come, you who are blessed by my Father; take your
inheritance, the kingdom prepared for you since the
creation of the world. For when I was hungry, you
gave me something to eat. I was thirsty and you gave
me something to drink. I was a stranger and you
invited me in. I needed clothes and you clothed me.
I was sick and you looked after me. I was in prison
and you came to visit me.*

Then the righteous will answer him, 'Lord, when did we see you hungry and feed you, or thirsty and give you something to drink? When did we see you a stranger and invite you in or needing clothes and clothe you? When did we see you sick or in prison and go to visit you?'

I tell you the truth, whatever you did for one of the least of these brothers of mine, you did for me.

Then he will say to those on his left, 'Depart from me, you who are cursed, into the eternal fire. For I was hungry and you gave me nothing to eat, I was thirsty and you gave me nothing to drink, I was a stranger and you did not invite me in, I needed clothes and you did not clothe me, I was sick and in prison and you did not look after me.

They also will answer, 'Lord, when did we see you hungry or thirsty or a stranger or needing clothes or sick or in prison, and did not help you?

He will reply, 'I tell you the truth, whatever you did not do for one of the least of these, you did not do for me.'

"I really gave it to the goats," Mike recalls. "I called them a bunch of hypocrites and sent them away. One woman thought I was really mad at her. I saw her walking away and had to call her back to let her know that it was just part of the performance."

Acting out the *Crucifixion*, Mike backed up to the cross Manolo had constructed for him. Raising his arms and looking up to the sky, he cried out into the open air of the plaza, *"My God, My God. Why have you forsaken me?"*

He slumped his head downward, feigning death. Silence came over the crowd. With the eyes of the audience glued to him, Mike lifted up his head.

"Do not be sad. Jesus is not dead. He is risen."

He walked over to an elderly man, putting his arm on the man's shoulder, "He is risen in you sir, with your experience and wisdom."

He then knelt down in front of a girl, "He is risen in you my young friend, with the boundless wonder in your eyes."

He shook a young man's hand, "He has risen in you. For when you fight for justice and truth, Jesus lives."

Mike walked back to his props and thanked the crowd for participating in the performance. The audience erupted with applause.

On the bus ride home that night, he was oblivious to the odd stares he had drawn earlier in the day. It had gone better than he could have ever imagined. He was riding a high from the performance, knowing he had shared the essence of the story that had inspired him as boy. He couldn't wait to do it again.

The performance would evolve over the next three and a half years. Mike tweaked different lines. *"Poor in spirit"* just became *"Poor"*, as he wanted to emphasize the squalor that surrounded the city. Larger crowds gathered to see him each week, as one could count on his performance every Thursday at noon, from January 1994 through October 1997.

There were some logistical hurdles that had to be worked out in the beginning. During one of his first performances, a concerned woman ran inside the Cathedral, exclaiming that there was a fake priest outside impersonating Jesus. A priest inside calmed the woman down and told her that he knew Mike and that the Church had given him their blessing. From then on, Mike made sure he announced before each performance that he was an American priest working with Maryknoll.

Stories about Mike were covered in the Chilean media and he received invitations from around the country to share his performance. In 1996, Mike was asked to perform for an elementary school in the city of Linares. The crowds in the plaza and other venues never exceeded a hundred or so people. As the children gathered in the auditorium in Linares, Mike peeked out from backstage. Six-hundred youthful faces were waiting for him to begin.

"I knew the performance like the back of my hand, but

this was bigger than anything I had done before."

Then Mike thought of the young man who had bravely acted out the agony of torture, and the adolescents he'd directed over the years. Most prominently, he remembered the children who had guided him through the poblaciones.

"The kids in the crowd were just like Carlito, Loreto, and Manolo. They had no ego to protect and everything was new. That energy gave me the courage to walk out there."

After his performance, he received a standing ovation.

"I was humbled. I had come a long way. If it weren't for *The Spirit*, I never would have imagined it."

From childhood on, Mike had steadily gone from being a shy boy, intimidated by the traditions of family, culture, and faith, to a man who thrived in the public forum — reflexively relying on an inner voice that drew him closer to a genuine existence.

"Those years were the culmination of everything I had learned in theater and life. In all the acting and directing I had done over the years, there was always something absent. Now with a spiritual message, there was a unity. The performance was about who I was and what I believed."

By the fall of 1996, the end of Mike's time in Chile was just over the horizon. His second five-year leave from the Syracuse Diocese would expire in less than a year. He still believed he was called to work overseas, but was unsure how his diocese would react to this notion. He thought of serving in other Latin American countries and even entertained ideas of another continent. Furthermore, he felt there were aspects of his character he had yet to explore. During his last year in Chile, his spiritual compass would point him in a new direction. A Chilean priest named Mariano Puga would provide the map.

Note: The Crucifixion scene described in this chapter is an amalgam of information provided by Father Mike, along with text that appeared in a 1994 Maryknoll Magazine article by Stephen DeMott. See Source Materials for details.

PART TWO

The Journey Inward

six

THE AUTHENTIC ARCHITECT
SANTIAGO — PINOCHET ERA

Padre Mariano Puga didn't know if it was day or night. He was blindfolded and handcuffed. The woman's screams from the jail cell down the hallway pierced his soul. For three days, his sunrise had been the sound of electricity coursing through the woman's central nervous system. His sun set when the apathetic voices of their jailers drifted away into a silent abyss.

Hung from her cell's ceiling, the woman's arms slowly and painfully dislocated from her shoulders. Burned and blistered, her vagina was the entry point of the electricity that forced out her deafening shrieks. Feeling of any kind in this most sacred part of her anatomy would unlikely ever return.

After listening to the woman's unending cries for mercy,

Mariano had run out of tears. It was the silence he dreaded. He knew that in a minute or an hour, her misery would begin again.

Mariano was never physically tortured, yet for a man who had spent his life honing the virtue of compassion, "...it was the worst torture anyone could have committed. I begged the Lord to put me in her place."

Twice a day, he opened his mouth like an infant, as the guards fed him slop. He ate it and always thanked them afterward. During the hours he spent alone, he said *The Rosary*, contemplating his improbable path to the jail cell.

Mariano was born into an elite Chilean family. His father, Mariano Puga Vega, was Chile's Ambassador to the United States from 1957 to 1959. Mariano came from a distinguished lineage of statesman, physicians, attorneys and engineers. His family had maintained wealth throughout the political and economic instability of twentieth-century Chile. Studying to be an architect in his early twenties, Mariano was set to start a respectable profession of his own — a career choice that would have ensured financial security for the rest of his life. In university, he was part of extracurricular study groups that analyzed Scripture and the writings of the Saints, St. Francis of Assisi in particular. During his last year of architecture school, he was part of a student group that ventured into the slums of Santiago to serve the poor.

"When I saw children rummaging through garbage piles," Mariano remembers, "I heard the call. I knew I wanted to live out the Gospels in the spirit of St. Francis."

In the months that followed his epiphany, Mariano broke off his engagement with his fiancé, quit school, and enrolled in the seminary. After being ordained in 1959, he spent two years in France studying and teaching theology. While in Paris, he was exposed to *The Worker Priest Movement*. Established in the early forties by Father Jacques Loew, the initiative sought to integrate priests into the everyday lives of laity. Laboring in factories or any other work environment was central to the movement.

Upon his return to Chile, Mariano served as Spiritual Director for the country's main seminary. In 1972, Mariano asked Cardinal Raúl Silva Henríquez if he and a group of priests could leave their parochial obligations to work in the copper mines north of Santiago, in Chuquicamata.

For a year, he and his colleagues worked as laborers alongside an uneducated and exploited workforce. When Pinochet came to power, Mariano was called back to Santiago. In the months after the coup, Mariano was indignant and spoke out against the regime despite the Chilean Church's initial support of Pinochet.

In June of 1974, Mariano was dragged from his bed in the middle of the night and bused to Villa Grimaldi, one of many edifices that had been converted into detention centers by Pinochet.

"There weren't the same numbers one might have seen in the Nazi concentration camps," Mariano recalls, "but the cruelty was the same."

After being released, the outraged priest vocalized what he had witnessed to Cardinal Silva.

"It was difficult for him (the Cardinal) to believe, but I also think he was deliberately aloof," Mariano recalls. "Holy men are not always saints. He eventually saw the truth and asked for my forgiveness."

The Cardinal then arranged a meeting between Mariano and Pinochet, so the priest could give a first-hand account of his experience. As a teen, Mariano had fulfilled an obligatory stint at one of the country's military academies. Pinochet had been a lieutenant to one of Mariano's older brothers.

"I had thirty minutes with the Generalissimo. He shook my hand and called me by my first name—like we were friends. I opened the conversation by saying, 'The first thing I was taught at the academy was that the orders of my superiors are never to be questioned. Generalissimo, my orders come from Jesus Christ. If I am not honest with you about what I have witnessed, I am disobeying those orders.'"

Pinochet listened intently and explained that if he were placed in Mariano's position, he too would be incensed. Pinochet said that during tumultuous times, mistakes are made. He told Mariano that he certainly didn't sanction what the priest had described and he would look into it. Mariano was encouraged. Pinochet suggested that the two should meet on a monthly basis to discuss what the priest was witnessing in the streets. Their first meeting would be their last. Mariano never met with Pinochet again. After several unreturned calls to the dictator's subordinates, Mariano realized the meeting had been a tactic to temporarily pacify the Church.

For the next quarter-century, Mariano lived in the slums of Santiago as a *Worker Priest*. He first labored as a truck loader and then, for the remainder of his time in the poblaciones, he painted anything that required a fresh coat. Most times he was paid for his work. For those who could not afford his services, he accepted food and shelter as payment. Throughout this time, he refused any income from the Church. The only time he did request financial help came in 1980, when he asked for assistance in buying a home.

"I want to live amongst the poor indefinitely," Mariano said to his superior. "But in order to continue my work, I need a home base."

"You're asking for a lot," his superior said.

"I understand, but I'm not looking for anything big. I just need a roof over my head."

"The most we can allocate is $3,000," his superior replied. "Is that enough?"

Mariano laughed. His colleague was naïve to the poverty of the poblaciones.

"The house I need to buy is only $400."

His superior reached into his pocket, handed Mariano $200, and told him he would have the rest by the end of the week.

Over the next two decades, Mariano dismantled and rebuilt the house several times as he moved from poblacion to poblacion. Between 1974 and 1989, Mariano was jailed seven times for his outspoken opposition to Pinochet.

When his cell door opened, Mariano was brought back to the present. It wasn't meal time. *What did they want?*

"So you're a priest?" the prison guard asked.

"Yes," Mariano answered, "but you better not let your fellow guards hear you talking to me. I'm a very dangerous man. Why do you think Pinochet would lock me up in a cell and make you feed me like a baby?"

"I don't know Padre, why?"

"Truth, son. I live the truth."

Mariano listened to the guard pace back and forth.

"I was wondering if you might help me," the guard said. "I'm getting married in a few months and my priest tells me I still have courses to complete before he'll marry us."

"But I told you, I'm an enemy of the state. Aren't you afraid I'll brainwash you?"

"I see the same things you see, Padre. I know all of this is wrong in the eyes of God."

"Then why are you here?"

"Because I need to make a living. I need to pay bills."

Mariano had taught theology at the seminary. In the slums he continued to read the works of theologians with whom he agreed *and* disagreed. One of his inspirations had been Chilean theologian Ronaldo Muñoz who said, "Jesus' meals with tax collectors shows the need to build, not burn bridges between the oppressed and the oppressors...excommunication was unnecessary, because those who partake in the Eucharist unworthily, eat and drink their own condemnation."

"What are the courses?" Mariano asked.

"I still have to complete a course on the *Sacraments* and another on *Male versus Female Psychology*."

Given what had transpired over the previous three days,

Mariano thought it unlikely that the guard would ever completely grasp the complexity of the opposite sex in a meaningful way.

"Alright, I will teach you the meaning of the *Sacraments*."

Mariano started with *Baptism*.

"I spoke to him like he was child." Mariano recalls. "With my eyes blindfolded, that's how I saw him."

Mariano knew how to articulate his faith in an intellectual manner. Yet after listening to a woman's involuntary propensity to live despite being mutilated, Mariano spoke from his heart. By the time he reached the *Sacrament of Matrimony* the following day, there were three other guards in the cell with him.

"When I stopped," Mariano recalls, "the guards said 'Please Padre, keep going. We want to hear more.'"

The woman's screams had subsided. Perhaps she had been released—or maybe Mariano's uniformed students were too busy listening to him to bother torturing her. He would never know. He just lived the truth.

SANTIAGO — 1996

Mike met Mariano during the protest years.

"He was such a stately looking figure," Mike recalls. "He stood 6'3 and had smoky white hair. A lot of times before protests, I wasn't sure if I understood the coded messages.

I would be walking down the street, thinking I was in the wrong place. Then I would see Mariano's white hair walking above the crowd and I was relieved."

The arc of Mike's Chilean tour was pitching downward by September of 1996. He had lived in Maryknoll-owned dwellings and with Chilean families for nine years. Mike asked Mariano if he could live with him in the poblacion of La Leuga for the remainder of his time in Chile.

"Of all the poblaciones," Mike recalls, "La Leuga was considered the most dangerous, but by that time, I thought I could handle it."

Mariano was skeptical whether Mike understood what it meant to live with him. Mariano's house, in the back yard of one of his parishioners, was at that point as dilapidated as the other shacks in the poblacion. He shared an outhouse with a family of seven.

"I told Mike, that when the wind comes blowing through this drafty old house in the winter, it's freezing. Sometimes people had a romantic idea of what it was like to live like me. I was afraid Mike didn't understand my lifestyle. Yet he never complained. What amazed me was how eager Mike was to share in the lives of the poor. I knew he was American, but by the time he came to live with me, he was Chilean."

Most days, Mariano and Mike were up at dawn for

Morning Prayer. For breakfast, they ate bread and drank tea. For the rest of the day, Mariano worked as any other person in the poblacion. Mike spent much of his time organizing theater groups, ministering to parishioners, and attending CBC meetings. At night, they sat by their kerosene heater and shared the stories of their lives.

Mariano told Mike that while the regime was still in power, he was always suspicious of new faces that showed up at his Masses.

"There were spies everywhere," he told Mike. "Masses were no exception."

A native of one of the wealthier sections of Santiago, Mariano often went back to visit his friends and family. Once, he was asked to give a sermon at a church in his old neighborhood. He noticed as he spoke, a handful of men got up and walked out. Leaving the church after Mass, Mariano was handcuffed and thrown into an unmarked car. He was charged with inciting subversive action.

"The sermon had no political agenda," Mariano told Mike. "I was simply describing how the poor lived and survived."

Mariano showed Mike what it was like to dedicate one's self to the poor without fear.

"He wasn't afraid of speaking truth to power," Mike recalls. "I didn't know it at the time, but it was a preparation.

I saw a deep spirituality in Mariano—not only a simplicity of faith, but a confidence that came from something deeper. I had stepped out of my comfort zone, but I wasn't where he was internally. He forced me to look inward. I had been focused on manifesting my faith outwardly. On those cold nights, I realized that I had to begin looking within myself."

Though they had known one another for years, Mike and Mariano had never said Mass together until Mike's year in La Leuga. Mike had grown accustomed to the impromptu fashion in which Mass often progressed in the poblaciones. Mariano took it a step further. When they said Mass together for the first time, there was no missal on the altar. Mike looked to Mariano, confused about what to do.

"I was good at ad libbing," Mike recalls, "but I still felt an attachment to the Liturgy."

Mariano began speaking to the congregation with an eloquence that made it appear as if he had memorized the Liturgy.

Mariano approached Mike after Mass and asked, "How long have you been a priest?"

"Twenty-two years."

"Michael, you know the essence of this by now. Let it come from *you*. Allow the spirit of the congregation to move you. You'll be more responsive to them. Be comfortable in what you have to offer them. You've earned it."

More than anything Mariano told Mike, it was the way in which the Chilean lived that convinced Mike a truly authentic life was possible. Mariano, almost twenty years older than Mike, was the embodiment of what he wanted to be. In the year he resided with his mentor, Mike would recall the words of St. Francis whenever he witnessed the deliberate and simple way Mariano lived — *Preach the Gospels at all times and when necessary use words.*

seven

SAFFRON DREAM
NEW YORK — 1997

On a trip home from Chile, Mike made his rounds, visiting friends and family. Though he enjoyed catching up with loved ones, the same discomfort he had felt after his trip to Mexico twelve years earlier, arose while he was home. He found it hard to imagine ever wanting to do anything besides live abroad, amongst populations as destitute as those in Santiago. Internally, he had made the decision that he no longer wanted to be on loan to Maryknoll. The choice was not entirely up to him though.

Mike made an appointment with Bishop James Moynihan at the diocesan home office in Syracuse. He spent an hour with Moynihan discussing his future. The Bishop saw value in Mike living abroad. Mike wrote articles for the diocese's newspaper, *The Catholic Sun*, about the people he had grown close to and the hardships they faced. The popular opinion with clergy in the diocese was that he made them proud and inspired their congregations. However, Moynihan gave no firm commitment when Mike asked to be released from the diocese to live the remainder of his life as a Maryknoller.

"We'll talk about it in a couple months," Moynihan said, knowing Mike would be back in October after he left Chile for good.

Mike walked out of the meeting feeling uneasy. Outside the Bishop's office, Mike ran into an old friend. Father Bobby Yeazel was the Bishop's assistant and responsible for prioritizing his obligations.

"So, how did it go Mike?" Yeazel asked.

"I don't know. I didn't get a clear answer."

"What's in your heart?"

"I want to be a Maryknoller for the rest of my life. There's no doubt in my mind that this is what I've been called to do."

Yeazel put an arm around Mike and said, "I'll see what I can do."

Within a week, Mike received a letter from the Bishop stating that he was released from all duties and obligations related to the Syracuse Diocese. Over the next ten years, Mike would continue to write articles and share his experiences when he made it home.

"I didn't want to break all ties with the diocese," Mike recalls. "I think that one of the great gifts of mission is to let people know what is happening on the other side of the world. I felt like I could give them a perspective they wouldn't get through other channels."

Before Mike left Chile in late September 1997, his friends and fellow clergy had a going away party for him.

"I asked him for his Bible," Claudio Escobar recalls. "It had tattered edges and Mike was always making notes in it."

"Why do want this old thing?" Mike asked.

"So someday I can give it to my children and tell them, 'This was the Bible of a saint.'"

Mike said goodbye to his other faithful friend and mentor, Mariano Puga.

"I was going to miss him," Mariano remembers. "My house felt so quiet after he left. I have been given many gifts as a priest. Michael Bassano is up there with my favorites."

From October 1997 through February 1998, Mike went through the process of becoming a permanent member of the Maryknoll Society. He attended classes and went through a battery of psychological testing to assure he was prepared for his next mission. During the process, Mike met with Father

Ray Finch, the Superior General of Maryknoll at the time.

"We have openings in Africa, Asia, and other South American countries. Brazil has some great ecclesial teams. Where do you see yourself?"

"I'm not sure," Mike said. "Can you give me some time to think about it?"

In Ossining, on the grounds of the Maryknoll campus resides a cloistered community of nuns who serve as spiritual advisors to missioners. Unsure of his next step, Mike turned to Sister Margaret Hawkins.

"I feel myself drawn to a more mystic path," he told the nun.

"It seems your life is moving in that direction, but you need to listen closely. Let *The Spirit* tell you."

A few days later, Mike awoke from a long night's rest with the certainty that had been eluding him.

"Saffron robes. That's what I saw," Mike remembers.

He had dreamt the night before, he was walking down a road with the skyline of a city in the background. In the distance he saw a grouping of hazy figures approaching. As they drew closer, he saw that they were Buddhist monks.

"I stopped in my tracks. They were talking to one another and when our paths crossed, they stopped too. They didn't say anything to me. They just smiled."

That morning, Mike got out of bed, walked over to Ray Finch's office, and told his superior, "I want to go to Thailand."

eight

THE PRINCE
BANGKOK, THAILAND — 1998-2000

Mike arrived in Bangkok on February 9, 1998. For the next ten months he attended language school.

"People always say to me, 'You have such a gift for learning languages,'" Mike says. "I wish they could have seen me while I was learning Thai. I was in tears at times. I was almost fifty and I just couldn't retain it. Every time I tried to speak Thai, Spanish kept coming out."

With forty-four consonants, sixteen vowels, and five variations of intonation, Mike was slow in grasping the language.

"There were a lot of times in that first year that I just wanted to leave," Mike recalls, "but I would spoil myself like I had in Chile. I would go to the movies and treat myself to some ice cream. Then I would sit on a park bench and have a good cry for myself. But I always went back to class the next day and kept trying."

One of Mike's teachers encouraged him to take an examination that, if he passed, would give him a certificate stating he had a sixth grade proficiency in Thai. He reluctantly agreed.

"I failed it miserably. I think I got a twenty out of a hundred. I was done with school. I told my teacher that I would learn the rest on my own. I'm the type of person where language has no meaning if I'm not with the people I want to communicate with. At the time, I was living at a Maryknoll house and it was comfortable by any standards. I knew that I wanted to live among the poor again. I felt that once I was living in the slums, I would get it."

While he was studying Thai, Mike had begun volunteering part-time at Mercy Centre, a multi-faceted organization founded by American-born priest Joe Maier of the Redemptorist order. Maier arrived in Klong Toey, a Bangkok port district of 120,000, in the early seventies. Maier set out to serve a Vietnamese population working in the filth and disease-ridden pork slaughterhouses that had made the slum infamous.

The willful killing of any sentient being is prohibited in Buddhism. Thailand is over 95% Buddhist. The small percentage of Muslims living in the slum refused to even touch pigs, as their faith would not allow it. For Vietnamese Catholics living in Klong Toey, the unsanitary slaughterhouses provided one of the only legitimate sources of income.

By the time Mike arrived at Mercy Centre, Maier had spent the previous twenty-six years sewing a seam of charity throughout the slum. He had built nursery schools, hospices, and an orphanage. On several occasions, he purchased back the freedom of children sold into the sex industry by their parents. Maier was a living legend to the poor of Klong Toey.

Prior to approaching Maier about working at Mercy Centre, Mike consulted with fellow missioners about the famed Father Joe. The feedback he received was that of qualified admiration. Maier had done wonderful things, Mike heard, but he also had a temper. Mike was warned that Maier's ego was to be reckoned with.

To his advocates, Maier's ego was necessary in serving an area besieged by gangsters, junkies and prostitutes. Over 70,000 children have learned to read and write in his nursery schools. He has been honored by the royal family of Thailand and other dignitaries—foreign and domestic. From what Mike observed in his time with Maier though, the aging priest was prone to outbursts. Mike found Maier overly defensive when his views or actions were called into question—often leaving those on the other end wondering whether Maier was a saint or a rogue. For those who knew Maier well, he was a bit of both.

"I was attracted to the work," Mike recalls. "I had done some AIDS ministering in Chile and knew Thailand was in crisis. I went in knowing that working with Joe would be a challenge, but I'd faced much more frightening things in the past."

Mike began volunteering full-time at Mercy Centre at the end of 1998. His duties were to minister to those dying of AIDS and help out at the orphanage. He found it difficult in the beginning to connect with the patients, as his Thai was still weak. His inability to consistently understand them made his first months at Mercy Centre a trial by fire.

"Some of the patients would get mad at me and lash out, calling me stupid," Mike recalls. "I understood their frustration. They were dying, and here I was, a stupid farang (foreigner) who didn't understand what they needed."

As he had done in Chile, Mike turned to music as a bridge in connecting with those he served and the community in which he now lived. On Saturday mornings, he walked the streets of Klong Toey with his guitar, singing nursery rhymes and pop songs he had learned in language school.

"The Thai culture was much more reserved," Mike recalls. "They wouldn't invite you into their houses like they did in Chile. Thai's felt ashamed of their living conditions and couldn't understand why a foreigner would want to be part of their lives. They peeked out their windows, wondering who I was. Kids have been my *in* no matter where I've travelled to. Kids love to have fun and music is always fun. After a couple weeks, they would all come running out. They taught me songs about sea creatures and asked me to play them over and over. I got to know their parents this way. "

Mike also took his guitar to the hospice. On one occasion, it was a song from Mike's youth that brought solace to Pompinon, a 49 year-old woman dying of AIDS. Mike went through his repertoire of Thai songs when Pompinon requested *Que Será Será*, the Doris Day classic. Pompinon's eyes lit up when Mike sang the song she had been taught by her mother as a little girl.

"The song brought her back to a time of innocence," Mike recalls, "She came to life when we sang it together. In her last days, she grew thinner and weaker. I could see that the lyrics took on new meaning for her. She was able to let go."

During the year Mike volunteered full-time at Mercy Centre his Thai improved, helping in his ministry with the orphans and patients. His relationship with Maier however, never reached a point where Mike felt Maier respected him.

"I felt limited in what I could do, other than to just be present and empathize with the patients," Mike recalls. "Joe and I would talk, but it always felt like there was an inequality to our relationship. At times, I felt that he didn't think I was doing anything of real value. But he never gave me any guidance on what he expected."

Tom Crowley, a volunteer for twelve years at Mercy Centre, says, "Back then people would tell Father Joe, 'I want to come and volunteer.' He would never turn them away, but then they would flounder. Most didn't speak Thai and the Thai staff was always suspicious of new people. Father Joe was like a professional hunter heading up an expedition with a bunch of amateurs stumbling behind him. He would say, 'Have at it.' But he had a real problem if you couldn't do it."

Crowley, a Vietnam War veteran and retiree, says now there is more clarity in what the centre expects from volunteers. "We tell people, 'Mercy is not going to adjust to you. You have to adjust to Mercy.' In Mike's defense, Mercy is a very hard place to fit in. You have to find a way to carve out value. Mike didn't have a clear vision and Father Joe wasn't going to hold his hand."

When Maier started out, missioners were thrown into the deep end of the pool with nothing. They had to build their own fiefdoms and were protective of what they had established. Asian mission work was different than what Mike had grown accustomed to in Chile, where virtually everyone was

Christian. Maryknoll historian, Father Michael Walsh, states that, "The guys in Asia, Africa, and South America are very different in their approaches to mission. They have to be."

Still, Mike felt Maier's impatience was counterproductive. Disconnect between the two men came to a head in early December 1999. Mercy Centre had gained international recognition for the strides Maier had made in bringing attention to the needs of Klong Toey's inhabitants. Public figures made high profile visits to the centre, raising awareness and generating funds necessary to sustain the operation. In late November 1999, news spread quickly through the centre that Prince Andrew of Great Britain would be visiting in a few weeks. The day before the Prince's arrival, Maier held a meeting where he laid out his expectations to staff and volunteers. At the end of the meeting, Maier pulled Mike aside and told him he expected to see Mike in his blacks the following day.

"I told Joe I hadn't worn a collar in twelve years and I wasn't going to change that for a prince." Mike remembers. "Joe walked away saying, 'I'll see you in your blacks tomorrow.'"

Maier, himself, rarely wore a collar except during public relations events such as this. The next day, Maier was hustling around the centre in his cassock, with Rosary beads hanging from his belt — the formal attire of Redemptorist priests. Mike was sitting at a bedside, wearing khakis and a short-sleeved dress shirt. Maier saw Mike from across the ward and made a beeline in his direction.

"He started pointing and shouting at me, saying he wanted me out. I stood up and we were nose to nose. I told him, 'I'm sorry Joe, but I don't live by any collar. What I do defines me, not what I wear.' Then I walked out."

Mike went back to work the next day. Neither he nor Maier discussed the argument.

"No one can deny the incredible impact Joe has had on the people of Klong Toey," Mike says, "but the unhealthy pride I saw in him turned me off. As I spent more time with the children and patients, they would tell him how much they liked me. I thought this was a sign that I was making progress. But I saw jealousy in Joe's eyes—like he was the only one who deserved praise. I was just trying to find a sense of worth in what I was doing, but I refused to walk on pins and needles, worrying whether Joe approved of me or not. Eventually, I realized that there was no way we were ever going to get along. I think Joe felt the same way."

On December 13, 1999, Mike attended a concert of Handel's *Messiah*.

"There's the part where they sing, '… and the glory of the Lord shall be revealed.' When I heard this, I began weeping.

An overwhelming sadness came over me. I felt like *The Spirit* had always guided me, but now I felt completely lost."

A week later, Mike came down with pneumonia. He went to the hospital on Christmas Eve morning and was given anti-biotics. He wasn't bedridden, but the doctor told him to take it easy. Mike was slated to say Midnight Mass that evening.

"I had a fever and was sweating," Mike recalls, "but after dinner that night, I thought I felt good enough to say Mass."

During the Second Reading, Mike passed out and fell off his chair. After a few moments, he came to and was taken home.

"Stress had left me open to getting sick," Mike says. "I was in bed for a week. I prayed and meditated, asking for guidance. I finally heard a voice inside saying, 'You have done your best, but now it's time to move on.' To where, I had no idea. I just knew that my current situation had to come to an end."

After he recovered, Mike notified Maier that he would be leaving. Seven years later, Mike and Maier ran into one another in a Bangkok mall. Maier was treating some of the kids from the orphanage to lunch. He and Mike made small talk for a few minutes. Before they said goodbye, Maier asked, "We've given ourselves up to the poor, haven't we Mike?"

"We certainly have, Joe," Mike replied.

It was a reconciliation of sorts. Mike felt that during those seven years after he had left Mercy Centre, Maier had thought as much about the meaning of their time together as he had.

Mike had come to Thailand with the inclination that his Asian experience would reveal a part of himself he had yet to explore. After almost two years, his adjustment to the language, culture, and work had proven thorny and more complex than he had imagined. Real growth is painful, and although he trusted that he still had something to offer, Mike left his first experiences in the country feeling he had failed. He pushed ahead though, hoping his next endeavor would open him up to a more harmonious understanding of himself. An unfolding would occur over the next three years. It would be a stage where Mike would grapple with facets of mission he found limiting.

"Those first five years in Thailand were painful, but *The Spirit* was still leading me. I didn't know it at the time. I do now."

nine

PALM TREE THEOLOGY
CHIANG RAI, THAILAND — 2000-2003

After leaving the Mercy Centre, Mike met with the Maryknoll team responsible for helping him discern where he would next serve. Maryknoll policy was to assess the strengths of a missioner, the needs of a community, and logistics. With approval from the unit coordinator, the missioner was then sent forth.

Maryknoll received word that a Spanish priest in the northern province of Chiang Rai was in desperate need of help. Father Roberto Garcia was the pastor of Blessed Sacrament parish in the village of Mae Suay. The parish included a church, a school a few miles away, and a dormitory for children ages five to nine. Father Roberto's duties extended outward from the parish, into twenty-seven hill tribes whose inhabitants consisted of immigrant populations that had illegally crossed over into Thailand from China, Laos and Myanmar (Burma) throughout the twentieth century. Father Roberto spent much of his time trying to formally naturalize Catholics of the hill tribes as citizens of Thailand.

The Thai government had long treated the tribes' people as second class citizens, as the lands they had squatted on were part of protected national forests. Christian missioners first arrived in Chiang Rai in significant numbers during the 1950s. Their presence was initially met with skepticism by the tribes' people. Yet as decades passed, missioners gained acceptance from tribal elders. They provided the tribes with medicines and taught them modern farming methods, extending life expectancy. In contrast to the way the Thai government had treated the tribes, missioners were seen as less of a threat to their culture's survival. Roughly thirty to forty percent of the tribes' people had converted from their animist belief system to Christianity by the end of the century.

Mike and his team agreed it would be a good opportunity for him. The prospect of engaging in interreligious dialogue with the Buddhist communities in Mae Suay was seen as a plus. Following a few phone interviews, Father Roberto invited Mike to serve with him.

Mike traveled 450 miles by train and bus from Bangkok

to Mae Suay. After settling in for a few weeks, a daily routine emerged. Mike's days began by leading the children of Blessed Sacrament in Morning Prayer and then seeing them off to school. From 9 a.m. to 4 p.m., he ministered to the sick and dying of Mae Suay at a local hospital with a group of nuns from the Camillus order. In the evening, he said Mass for the parish's children. On weekends, he ventured off into the hills.

"It was a completely different existence from anything I had ever experienced," Mike remembers. "It was rural and many didn't speak Thai. The Akha and Lahu people spoke indigenous languages (also called Akha and Lahu)."

It was the time Mike spent going from village to village, celebrating Mass, he found most rewarding. He identified with their simple way of life and lack of desire for material wealth. During his first year in the hills, he made regular visits to the Akha village of Hoay Ya Sai. The tradition for visitors who entered the grounds of any village was to first visit with tribal elders. Hoay Ya Sai's tribal elder was Adhong, an aging man who didn't speak Thai. During Mike's first few visits, the priest was not accompanied by a catechist to translate for him. Adhong's son, Aja, spoke Thai but he was sent out into the farming areas to notify his fellow Catholics whenever Mike arrived. This left Mike and Adhong alone, a gaping language barrier between them.

"Adhong always had a big smile on his face," Mike remembers. "Only a few teeth, but a big smile. We would sit there for an hour sometimes, just looking at each other. Adhong would say, 'Michael'. Then I would say, 'Adhong.' We would laugh and after a few minutes the laughter would die down. Then he would repeat my name and I would repeat his and we would laugh again. We taught each other songs. Neither of us understood each other. It didn't matter. We were communicating in melodies."

On Easter Sunday, a year later, Mike was present when Adhong made the *Sacrament of Confirmation*. The village celebrated and the two men shared a few cups of rice liquor, again just calling out each other's names and laughing.

At 66 years-old, Adhong spent much of his day in the hut he shared with his son, daughter-in-law, and grandchildren. Adhong passed the time by drinking, a habit not popular with his daughter in-law. Following a quarrel one night, his family went to bed. The next morning Adhong was found hanging from one of the beams in his hut.

"I think he saw himself as a burden," Mike remembers. "I was saddened he wouldn't be there to greet me anymore. He taught me how important it is to call someone by name. There's an inherent respect in doing this, regardless of how close you are to someone. I would always remember that gift."

"My Christmas's in the hills were special," Mike remembers.

On Christmas Eve, during his second year in Mae Suay, Mike and some others from the parish drove into the hills to celebrate Vigil Mass in one of the villages.

"Their chapel was simple. It had a thatched roof and bamboo walls. The pews were made out of tree stumps. I had to laugh when I saw their manger. They had apparently been given a baby doll years earlier that served as Jesus. They built a manger, but it was barely big enough for the doll. We stuffed it in there anyway."

The candlelit Mass began at 9 p.m. When it concluded, the celebration began.

"We went from hut to hut," Mike recalls, "carrying the baby Jesus, crammed in his little manger. People gave one another gifts and we ate and drank. We went to twenty homes that night. By three in the morning, I was exhausted. They knew how to throw a party."

Looking up at the sky, blanketed with stars not dimmed by city lights, Mike remembers thinking that Christmas morning, *"This is the closest I might ever come to experiencing what it was like two-thousand years ago."*

MR. FATHER

During Mike's first year in the hills, he and Father Roberto got along well enough. Father Roberto was more traditional than Mike in his approach to mission, but Mike felt their common goals outweighed their philosophical differences. Their relationship would sour though. Mike's approach to service, as well as who he was as at his core, would ultimately be called into question by his colleague.

Whenever Mike had some free time, he wandered the flora canopied roads outside the parish. Up the hill from the church, he came across a Buddhist temple. He waved to the monks of the temple and they waved back, in the same manner he had dreamt about prior to coming to Thailand. On subsequent strolls up the road, he conversed with the monks and they invited him to their festivals.

"We never spoke about religion," Mike recalls. "We just broke bread together and tried to connect in a meaningful way. They were my neighbors."

As a Maryknoller, Mike felt a dialogue through friendship was a positive effort that set a good example for the children of the parish.

"I felt our relationship was constructive. I invited them down to the parish, but that never materialized. I also spoke to the children at the school about my visits and they told me they wanted to come with me. That never happened either."

130

Following Mass one day, Father Roberto told Mike he had been hearing some unsettling talk.

"I hear you've been spending time up on the hill."

"I have," Mike replied. "I went to the Visakah Puja celebration (Buddha's birthday) last week."

"Some of our staff has come to me asking why a Catholic priest would spend time with monks, worshipping Buddha."

Mike grinned, uncertain if his colleague was serious. Father Roberto maintained a staid expression.

"Now Roberto, we both know that no one worships Buddha in the Christian sense," Mike said. "Buddha said he was simply one who was awakened. These monks are kind men and I've built a friendship with them."

"But Mike, you need to understand that this sort of behavior confuses the children. We're trying to teach them that Jesus is their savior, not Buddha."

"I think you underestimate the capacity for understanding and love these kids have."

"We are Christians Mike—not Buddhists. We're here to serve the Christian population."

"These men hold no ill will towards us or what we're doing. We aren't competing with them. Are you implying we're better than them?"

The conversation went around in circles. The two

clergymen agreed to disagree for the time being.

"Roberto had some very clear objectives," Mike recalls. "It took me awhile to realize these were written in stone. As kids, we were told that if we went into a Protestant Church, it was a sin. I thought the old days were over."

Mike found himself gradually isolated from the staff at the parish. Another Spanish priest, Father Antonio Cedillo, came to the parish during Mike's second year in Mae Suay. Mike learned quickly that Antonio shared Roberto's resistance to deviating from traditional missionary objectives. Mike's carefree attitude and acceptance of the world as something that didn't need to be fixed was viewed as an affront by his colleagues.

From the time Mike had been ordained, he had seen that his words and actions were most effective when he put himself on an equal plane as those he served. As a child, he had been intrigued by the stature priests had been given in the hierarchy of the Church. As he grew older, those impressions faded. He saw that meaningful service was grounded in compassionate action rather than ritual and dogma.

In homilies geared toward children, Mike had always come down from the pulpit to speak to his young congregations. He felt whatever the message was, it resounded more clearly when he was closer to them. At Blessed Sacrament, the congregation was virtually all children and he continued this practice.

"I didn't talk about sin or hell or the devil," Mike remembers. "I wanted them to know how much God loved them. Did the children like this? It appeared to me they enjoyed it. I was speaking to them on a more personal level."

Father Roberto and Father Antonio had more traditional approaches to their homilies.

"I respected them. That was their style," Mike says. "I thought maybe it was a good balance. They didn't."

On one occasion, Mike and Father Antonio were walking the kids to church, when one of the children asked Mike, "Do you think there is a hell?"

Mike thought for a moment and said, "You know, I believe that God is too compassionate and loving for there to be a hell. I do think that some of the things people say, or the way they act, can create a hell for themselves and those around them. This is just as bad."

The child began to ask another question. Father Antonio interrupted, "Father Mike, if you don't believe in hell, then there is something very wrong with you."

The two men exchanged glares and continued on to the church in silence.

Ralph Maughan, a retired fireman and Maryknoll lay

missioner, visited Mike twice in Mae Suay. Ralph observed what Mike's modesty would never allow him to admit.

"I think Mike was *too* liked by the villagers and children," Ralph says. "I think the other two priests were jealous and felt threatened by him. Mike is so genuine and happy all the time and they thought he was too good to be true. So they started looking for flaws."

During Mike's second year in the hills, another individual was brought into the mix. A Filipino lay missioner, David Bituin, designated himself as the one who would tell Mike how he should act. The two had met when Mike first arrived in Thailand. David had established a mission sending group from his home diocese in the Philippines and connected with Maryknoll Thailand. David had heard about Mike's dramatization of *Matthew* in Chile. Mike went to the Philippines to perform at David's home parish. A few years later, David decided to become a long-term lay missioner and because Blessed Sacrament was understaffed, Maryknoll put him in contact with Father Roberto.

"I thought we were friends," Mike remembers, "but once he got up in the hills, everything changed."

David was assigned to chaperone the children of the parish when they went to school. He made sure they were up and ready in the morning and helped the children maintain an orderly environment in the parish dormitory. He worked hand in hand with the parish's schoolmaster, a Thai woman, Kanya, who had once told Mike, "You need to start acting more like a priest."

"I was never a disciplinarian," Mike recalls. "From the time I was a child, I didn't see the *'Do this or else…'* approach as effective. Thailand is a monarchy, so there is a long tradition of hierarchy in the society. Kanya's impression was that, because I was a priest, I needed to act in an authoritarian way. All the years I had been working with kids, and my experiences growing up, told me that this approach may work temporarily, but it leaves kids with a resentment they carry into adulthood. Also, I didn't wear the collar. I think subconsciously, the staff saw me as lower in status to Antonio and Roberto."

Shortly after David's arrival, he took an attitude similar to Mike's colleagues.

"You need to listen to me, Mike" David said. "I'm Asian and you're in an Asian culture and you are expected to act a certain way."

"And what way is that?"

"These kids are young and need direction. They look up to you and you aren't fulfilling your role. You're not setting a good example for the priesthood or for what Maryknoll represents."

Mike was enraged. He had admirably served as a Maryknoller for fourteen years.

"What did this guy know about me? He wasn't even a Maryknoller." Mike recalls thinking. "I didn't want to go into who had more credentials in service. That would have been egotistical. I was furious, so I ended the conversation with one word — Bullshit!"

David went to Father Roberto and told the pastor of the dispute. Roberto called a meeting.

"We had a heated discussion," Mike recalls. "It was apparent that I had a different outlook than everyone else in the parish, but differences in opinion are what drive any organization forward. The Church has been in transition for two-thousand years. I wanted a positive discourse and was willing to be flexible as long as it didn't mean surrendering up my integrity. I still believed that something positive could come from it."

The situation continued to deteriorate. David and Kanya gave Mike the silent treatment. When Mike said Mass, they refused to take Communion from him.

"The kids noticed these things," Mike recalls. "The last thing I wanted to do was involve them. I was in a situation where the clergy and staff barely recognized my existence."

Naturally, Mike began to question himself. Again, he turned to his spiritual advisors. Father Dan Fagan, a Franciscan psychologist, met with Mike once a month at a retreat house in Chiang Mai. Mike spoke of his alienation in the parish. They discussed the possibilities of why this challenge was presenting itself now. Mike had been struggling for most of his adult life with expectations regarding stature and role. In Mae Suay, Mike wrestled with maintaining a sense of self in an environment wrought with pettiness.

"I had to start asking myself," Mike recalls. "'What do I stand for in relationship to service?' I had to come to terms with my issues regarding role."

Looking for guidance, Mike frequently called friends in Bangkok and the States. They heard an uncharacteristic depression in his voice. Mike then turned to Sister Margaret, his trusted spiritual advisor in Ossining.

"I encouraged Mike not to succumb," Sister Margaret recalls. "The external pressure didn't make sense to him, and for good reason. There was a wisdom at work within him. His way of communing was to be at one with the people, where there was a basic respect and understanding, and all things were equal. That is where Mike had found his greatest joy. The traditional confines that seemed to be the focus at his parish were separating him from this communion. He was being asked to give up a part of himself that restricted the wonderful energies he had to offer. Certainly building churches and schools, as Maryknoll and other organizations have done over the years, has its merits. It has its limitations too. It has to go deeper than that and Mike knew this. But everyone around him was telling him different. When we focus too much on projecting our own beliefs onto others, we diminish the ability of people to explore the depths of their own spirituality. Mike knew this intuitively and I believe he was brought to that place in time so that he could confront his issues with role and status. He was being called to move through it, into an existence where these restrictions could melt away—where he could become a more fully realized instrument of compassion."

Unbeknownst to Mike at the time, David had written a letter to a Maryknoll missioner living in China. He complained that Mike was a nuisance and disrupting the parish. He told the missioner that the priests of Blessed Sacrament were questioning their association with Maryknoll and that something had to be done. It wasn't long before word got back to Maryknoll's unit coordinator in Bangkok.

"What's going on up there?" Mike's superior asked him in an unexpected call.

"We're having some differing opinions," Mike said, "but

we're working on it and I'm hopeful it can be resolved."

Mike felt as though there were uncontrollable forces at work, set on driving him out of the parish.

"I was kind of losing it at that point," Mike remembers. "Word got back to me that Maryknoll New York had been notified. I was also told that someone from Bangkok was on their way up to investigate. Dan Fagan came through for me. He was ready to strangle someone. He wrote a letter to New York saying, 'I'm a psychologist. Mike is fine. There is major dysfunction within his team.' Thank God he wrote that letter, because I thought I was going crazy."

In November 2002, a Maryknoll priest made a trip to Mae Suay to assess the situation. After listening to grievances from all the parties involved, Mike's colleague sat him down.

"They say you're immature."

Mike bit his tongue and listened.

"I'm going to leave the choice up to you, Mike. They say they are willing to try to work things out, but from what I've heard, I'm not sure this can work."

Mike deliberated in the weeks that followed. He didn't want to leave. He loved travelling to the hill tribes and sharing in a simple, but deep faith. A connection to the children was affirmed every time he brought smiles to their faces. Nevertheless, the awkwardness he felt from staff and clergy left him dejected. After thorough contemplation, Mike wrote in his journal:

> *Discernment is complete*
>
> *Called to move on now*
>
> *Not sure where the journey leads*
>
> *No longer worrying about the where or how*
>
> *Rejoicing in the present moment*
>
> *A gift enough to receive*
>
> *Guided by inner authority*
>
> *Worth trusting to believe*

Mike decided he would leave Blessed Sacrament after the holidays. He waited until a few weeks before he left to tell the students he was departing.

"There's an older priest in Bangkok who's sick and they need me down there," he told his young friends.

His colleagues honored him with a dinner, saying nice things about him. Beneath the compliments, Mike felt an attitude of—*Don't let the door hit ya' in the ass.*

"The dinner was like a morgue," Mike recalls.

In Chile and the States, he was always given tearful send-offs where he felt his efforts were appreciated. He knew that he had commendably served the parish and the hill tribes, but he was leaving under less than amiable terms.

"I felt like I just didn't fit in. I didn't know if I would ever fit in anywhere in Thailand," Mike remembers.

He would have to begin again, walking into a miasma of uncertainty. He hoped his commitment to compassion and recollections of perseverance would carry him through. He awoke early one morning, shortly after the New Year, gathered his few belongings and walked over to Father Roberto's office before Morning Prayer.

"I want you to know, Roberto," Mike said. "I leave here with my head held high. My integrity remains intact."

Walking off the grounds, Mike turned around to take one last look at the place he had served for close to three years. Colossal palm trees towered above the parish, their leaves dancing in the morning breeze. Gazing upward, Mike drew inspiration from their stalwart example, saying to himself, *"You have weathered many more storms than me and you still stand strong — I will do the same."*

ten

THE TEMPLE'S ROAR

BANGKOK AND LOPBURI — 2003

Mike returned to the levitating smog and relentless noise of Bangkok. His superior assigned him to prison ministry. He spent the next six months visiting with a multi-cultural array of foreigners snagged smuggling drugs in and out of the country.

Bangkok was, and continues to be, a main hub for drug trafficking in Southeast Asia. Many prisoners were able to bribe their way out of long sentences, but those who could not afford it, sat in Thai jails, watching their lives dissipate. Most hoped they would be shipped back to their home countries to serve out the remainder of their confinement, part of international prisoner exchange treaties. The convicts Mike visited were disproportionately women who had served as mules for drug cartels in their home countries. He listened as the women, usually from poor backgrounds, told him how they were promised a year's salary for a few days work. Mike consoled them as they cried for their families. He gave them stamps so they could send letters home and brought magazines to help pass the time. His fluency in English and Spanish kept him busy with Europeans, North Americans, and Latinos. Still, he knew attempting to convince them that their mistakes were forgivable was not his calling. Also upon his return, Mike reluctantly conceded to get counseling per the advice of his superiors.

"I think they were looking for something more than what I had explained," Mike recalls. "I'd been talking to Dan Fagan and Sister Margaret throughout the ordeal in Mae Suay and was completely honest. I was moving toward a reflective type of life that came from a deeper source. A new counselor meant I had to relive the whole thing. I didn't feel that analyzing it was going to get me anywhere. I agreed to it though, and tried to remain open."

Mike spent much of the first half of 2003 focused on what German Zen Master, Karlfried Graf Durckheim, called being "transparent to transcendence." Through daily meditation and journaling, he entered into a period of deep introspection. He contemplated the words of the Sufi mystic, Rumi, and Vietnamese Buddhist monk, Thich Nhat Hanh. In doing so, he began to see himself as part of a larger truth, devoid of any label.

The temporal illusions of institution and title (i.e. the Church and priest) fell to the side as eternal truths awoke in Mike. If someone wished to define him as a Catholic priest or missioner, so be it, but he was first and foremost a servant to the spirit, teachings, and way of living exemplified by Jesus and Buddha. He knew the trivial aspects within organizations would always be present. More importantly, he understood the success of any mission group relied on facilitating an inclusive awareness of the divine. He vowed never again to appease manipulative personalities bent on projecting contrived agendas.

"A new confidence arose in me following my time in Mae Suay," Mike recalls. "I could no longer apologize for who I was or what I stood for."

Mike was satisfied that he was moving in the right direction spiritually, but questioned whether there was anywhere in Thailand where his gifts would be useful. He confided in friend and fellow Maryknoller, Father Frank Fielding. Fielding had spent the previous decade working alongside Buddhist monks, serving Burmese refugees fleeing a violent military junta in power since 1962.

"I sensed Mike wasn't particularly happy," Fielding remembers. "He always had a joyous way and exuberance about life. But when he returned to Bangkok, he appeared lost. When I explored this with him, he told me that he felt he just didn't fit in anywhere. I saw his experiences at Mercy Centre and Mae Suay as strong indications that *The Spirit* was calling him elsewhere. They weren't reflections of who he was as a person. *The Spirit* was simply pushing him toward something else. I suggested he look into the AIDS hospice I had visited ten years earlier."

After serving in Cairo and Beirut during the 1980s, Fielding arrived in Bangkok in 1990. He was uncertain of how he might fit into a Buddhist culture as comfortable with their religious tradition as Muslims were in the Middle East.

Fielding had earned a nursing degree in the early sixties before he joined the Maryknoll Society. Seeing as Thailand was quickly becoming the *Typhoid Mary* of the Asian AIDS crisis, Fielding thought his nursing skills would serve the country's growing HIV population. In 1992, Fielding took a trip to Lopburi, a town ninety miles north of Bangkok. He heard a Buddhist monk, Pra Alongkot Dikkapanyo, had begun taking in the discarded victims of the epidemic into his temple.

"There was very little understanding when it came to contraction, prevention and treatment of HIV/AIDS in Thailand in the early nineties," Fielding remembers. "Thais reacted much in the same way Americans reacted in the eighties. They were terrified."

Although the U.N. and the Thai government had aggressively funded programs to educate the public about contraction of HIV/AIDS, the dissemination of fact was drowned out by fearful misinformation, a societal reaction inherent to all epidemics. HIV/AIDS blew through the sex industry and drug culture of Thailand like a biological hurricane. An incorrect correlation was drawn by the Thai public that the disease was only contracted by addicts, homosexuals, and prostitutes. Those who suspected they were HIV positive avoided getting tested for fear of stigmatization. Husbands and wives passed it onto one another. Mother's transmitted the disease to their offspring *in utero*.

The U.S. had dealt with the initial stages of the AIDS outbreak with similar ignorance and fear. However, when Magic Johnson and Arthur Ashe announced that they had contracted HIV via non-homosexual or drug related behavior, HIV/AIDS was recognized as an imminent threat to all segments of society. Encouragement to be tested and blunt education in Europe and North America was standard as the millennium approached. Unfortunately, misinformation remained prevalent among most third world populations.

When Fielding walked into Prabhat Namphu Temple, the smell of bile, excrement, and decay nearly knocked him off his feet. The patients laid on mats waiting to die. It was not what one would consider a conventional hospice. There was no morphine to ease patients into death or doctors to oversee their care. The dying were abandoned by mothers, fathers, husbands, and wives, too ashamed to care for them in their last days. Other than the monks, the only attention paid to the patients came from flies that swarmed their oozing sores. Those who chose to help Pra Alongkot would not touch the dying. Instead, they used tree branches to push bowls of rice and water to the patients, believing they were maintaining a safe distance from infection. Fielding left the rudimentary operation in 1992, uncertain if his nursing skills could serve the dying in any meaningful way. Yet the temple in Lopburi remained in the back of his mind for the next decade. He had heard the initial operation had grown and that Pra Alongkot had worked out many of hospice's initial problems. By early summer 2003, Fielding felt confident enough to recommend the temple to Mike.

Mike walked onto the grounds of Prabhat Namphu

Temple without expectation. He was given a tour of the facility by Dr. Thomas Renard, a German physician who had been volunteering full-time at the temple for two and a half years. Renard had seen over two-thousand Thais succumb to the ravages of AIDS in varying forms (pneumonia, toxoplasmosis, meningitis, tuberculosis, and other opportunistic parasites, bacteria, and fungi). The volume of death from the day Pra Alongkot had opened its doors was evidenced in the seven-thousand cotton bags of cremated remains, stacked before a statue of the Buddha. The five-foot wall of white bags looked like a flood barricade, with the Buddha peering over its cloth horizon. On each bag was written the name of the deceased, along with the date and time they had expired. Mike walked through a thirty-three bed ward occupied by patients closest to death. He watched as volunteers and staff aided the patients.

"At Mercy Centre," Mike recalls, "my work was about being present to HIV patients. I didn't do any hands-on care. At the temple I saw volunteers changing diapers and showering people. I saw an opportunity to actually put my life at the service of another."

Before his initial visit to the temple, Mike told himself that the trip would just be a fact finding mission. Ambivalence vanished after what he saw, and when he returned to Bangkok the next day, he wrote in his journal:

> *Decisive time to act and move ahead*
>
> *Casting off all fear, criticism or dread*
>
> *Trusting completely in You*
>
> *The center of all I am and do*
>
> *The moment has arrived, inspired to let go*
>
> *Of anything that would impede The Spirit's flow*
>
> *Taking control of my life and well-being*
>
> *A deeper insight of mission, I am at last seeing*
>
> *New path clearly opened and choosing to take a stand*
>
> *Gently reaching out, grasping the Beloved's hand*

By summer's end, Mike was stationed full-time at the temple. Each weekday morning, he rode his bicycle from his guest house through the lush green hills of Lopburi, en route to the temple.

Like anyone starting a new job, he was tentative at first. He watched the staff and volunteers clean up vomit and feces. They carried out corpses to the hospice's eight crematoriums. During his first week, Mike got a wake-up call to precisely how hands-on his work would be.

"Could you change bed number five's diaper?" one of the

staff members asked him.

Initially, it was difficult for Mike to distinguish a patient's gender, either because their heads were shaved or their bodies were so wasted away. Mike was certain that bed number five was occupied by a female patient. He walked back to the staff member to notify her that she must have been mistaken.

"That's a woman," he said.

"We don't have enough help here. You're going to have to clean men *and* women."

"Oh, of course," Mike replied, trying to think of how to go about the task in a dignified manner.

Mike thoroughly wiped the woman's anus and put a clean diaper on her. The woman put the palms of her hands together, raised them up and bowed her head slightly, thanking him.

"Service arises from need," Mike says. "That is what needed to be done. I was very gentle and conscious that she felt as uncomfortable as I did. Yet I moved forward with reverence because she needed me at that moment."

One day, during his first month, Mike was toweling a male patient's feet dry after a shower when Scripture came to life.

Mike says, "During the Last Supper, Jesus said, '*If I then, your Lord and Teacher, have washed your feet; you also should wash one another's feet.*' It was Jesus' ultimate call to serve others with humility. *The Gospel of John* came alive for me that day and every time I washed a patient's feet thereafter."

In the months that followed, Mike settled into a routine of satisfaction. When he arrived in the morning, he changed diapers, applied Vaseline to chapped lips, poured water down parched throats, and shaved heads. Lice and scabies were a nuisance Mike caught three times in his first two years. He grew comfortable in his new work environment, making a point of remembering patients' names.

"*Good morning, Chen.*"

"*Can I get you a drink Wilapon?*"

"*Amphan, time for a shower.*"

Mike says now, "I wanted them to know that even though they had been stigmatized, calling out their names still signified they were alive. They were people, not a diagnosis."

The patients knew Mike was a holy man of some sort. Yet the way in which he helped them took precedence over his religious background. He did not wear the robes of the monks nor did he preach his faith to them at any point during their interaction. They called him *Khoon Pauw* — Mr. Father.

After years of service at the temple, Dr. Thomas Renard was dubious of volunteers' intentions. He felt many volunteers, mostly Westerners, had come to the temple for narcissistic reasons. Most didn't speak Thai and many left early because they didn't want to deal with the sordid tasks required in aiding patients. Yet they departed with their pictures of the dying, like ticket stubs — proof they had wallowed in the suffering of others. Dr. Thomas saw something different in Mike.

"He was completely consumed with the work from the first day," Thomas recalls. "He took on the worst tasks right away and never complained. The whole day he was like a ticking clock. Patients smelled horribly and could be unkind in their suffering. Mike didn't care. He just kept going. He was working in the same spirit as Mother Teresa."

What struck Dr. Thomas as odd was that Mike didn't seek out camaraderie or validation with any of the staff or volunteers. He admits, that after close to two years of working alongside Mike, he never really got to know him on a personal level.

"He was only concerned with patients," Dr. Thomas says.

Mike found completeness in tending to the immediate needs of the suffering. Intimate contact brought an understanding of healing that gave Mike the sense of purpose he had been yearning for since he had first arrived in Thailand. Through gentle touch, he felt the transference of healing energy, benefitting both he and the patients.

"The psychological healing that took place when I held someone's hand was incalculable," Mike recalls. "Most patients would never see their relatives again. Only ten-percent of families came back for patients' funerals, let alone to visit. When I caressed their forehead or massaged their legs, they no longer felt alone. Just by treating them with dignity, they felt worthy. Sometimes this gave them the strength to keep fighting. Other times it was this validation that allowed them to let go, knowing in their last moments that someone cared."

For the over seven-hundred patients who died during his time at the temple, Mike was, most often, the last face they saw before they let out their last breath.

His work was demanding. Mike was a healthy 55 year-old man, but he was still 55. The unlimited pools of energy he had expended without thought as a young priest ran low when he pushed himself. He tried not to take home the heaviness of temple. The exertion of riding his bike through the hills after a long day helped relieve tension. When he arrived home, he rested, meditated, journaled, and watched T.V. As he dozed off to sleep, he made a habit of reciting the words of poet Mary Anne Radmacher.

> *Courage does not always roar.*
> *Sometimes courage is the quiet voice at the*
> *end of the day saying,*
> *'I will try again tomorrow.'*

eleven

THE MONK AND THE BUTTERFLY
PRABHAT NAMPHU TEMPLE — 2003-2007

Mike says that he received as much as he gave to patients of the temple. By walking along a ridge between life and death, he was able to see the true nature of humankind. His payment came in smiles, thank you's, and the affection he received from those who were able to forget their suffering, if only for a little while. Though death was always an unwelcome guest, the wisdom of the dying provided him with a new understanding of mortality. For Mike, the duality of life and death gradually diminished as the months passed. He sensed a tangible, yet inexplicable, continuum when patients transitioned from form to spirit. This allowed him not to get caught up in eventualities, granting him the ability to appreciate the lessons each patient offered before they moved on.

The concept of mutual compassion, present in all religions, was most evident in Mike's relationship with an ex-convict named Bunserpa. Bunserpa was a weathered soul who had spent ten years in a Bangkok prison for dealing heroin. The skin that hung from Bunserpa's deteriorating physique was covered in tattoos.

Thai convicts, like those of most other prison cultures, puncture their dermis with ink as a way of expressing their reasons for being incarcerated and their affiliations with criminal elements. It is an unsanitary process. Prisoners use and reuse unsterilized sewing needles, guitar strings, and pens for their permanent etchings.

Bunserpa's markings, some artful, others chicken scratch, sent a message to patients that the 46 year-old man had resided in a place, perhaps, more daunting than the temple. When Mike walked into the hospice in the morning, Bunserpa sat up in his bed to let the priest know he was ready to go for a walk.

"He really didn't need much help," Mike recalls. "I think he just enjoyed the ritual of having someone present when he made his rounds."

When conversing with patients in his crotchety voice, Bunserpa would dismissively shake his head, responding to their complaints with an air of, *C'mon, that's nothing compared to the shit I've dealt with.*

After two years of staving off death, Bunserpa began to spiral down. In his last days, he was moved to a bed close to the nurse's station.

"When patients started slipping, their needs changed," Mike recalls. "They stopped eating, lost mobility, and began to fall away. Their needs became more spiritual."

After being moved, Bunserpa laid in his bed, observing the goings-on of the ward.

"It was a busy day," Mike recalls. "We were short staffed and I was running around, trying to keep my head above water."

The dying man noticed that no one ever asked Mike if he needed anything. Bunserpa lifted his arm and got Mike's attention as the priest buzzed by his bed. Mike pivoted and came to his bedside.

"Can I get you something? A drink?" Mike asked.

"I need nothing. Just come closer," Bunserpa whispered.

He grasped Mike's wrists, lifting his caretaker's hands to either side of his ink covered face.

"He didn't say anything. He just stared into my eyes." Mike recalls. "Then he began to gently massage my hands. It was the only thing he could give me. He did it with such care and deliberation. He reminded me that the only thing we can do is to give and receive with dignity. That was the gift I was present to every day."

The long list of tasks that had occupied Mike's mind moments before, vanished as he surrendered to Bunserpa's loving kindness. The two men just sat together. Mike had spent his entire adult life searching for a place that would allow him to serve without ego. Bunserpa had spent his life destroying himself with drugs and criminal behavior. Their paths to the temple could not have been more dissimilar. Yet their spirits converged at exactly the right moment for the two men to recognize their shared divinity.

Bunserpa saw that Mike was needed by other patients. After letting go of Mike's hands, he put his palms together and bowed his head.

"You have been a blessing to me, Mr. Father. Thank you. "

With a renewed sense of mission, Mike returned to the blessed task of serving the other patients. Bunserpa died hours later.

Pisanu was a middle-aged man who arrived at the temple after spending seven years in bed. He had suffered a stroke at the age of thirty. Except for partial use of his right hand, the rest of his right side was left paralyzed. The stroke was initially thought to be independent of any underlying disease. As the years passed though, he would develop other symptoms. Eventually, he tested positive for HIV.

His family, ashamed, did little else besides feed him. Pisanu rotted away. Staring at the ceiling of his bedroom, he longed for the days when he was still able to put one foot in front of the other. When he was 37 years-old, Pisanu's family gave up on him. They dropped him off at the temple and never came back.

At 6'2, Pisanu was tall for any culture, let alone that of Thailand. Once at the temple, regular meals and care allowed him to put on weight. An outgoing personality began to emerge and his assertive demands for food and drink were seen as positive signs.

Pisanu surprised Mike one day by saying, "I want to walk!"

Mike was pleased and thought, *"If he wants to walk he has hope, and if he has hope, then he wants to live."*

Known to the staff as a man of the cloth, Mike was still just a volunteer at the temple. To do anything out of the ordinary with a patient required approval from Dr. Thomas. Mike approached the physician and told him of Pisanu's desire.

"No," the physician said. "He's paralyzed. He'll hurt himself."

"But it's his will. Can I just try to get him out of bed?"

Dr. Thomas had developed a thick skin to the unlikely. It was a logical coping mechanism. Demise was a stark reality, confirmed by the thousands of dead bodies he had witnessed leaving the hospice. Nonetheless, Mike could not ignore the resolve in Pisanu's voice, and the priest persisted.

"I'll hold him," Mike said, "and if he falls back, I'll put him back in bed and it's over. But can we at least we give him a try?"

Dr. Thomas acquiesced, but told Mike, if Pisanu was hurt, the priest would be held responsible.

It was not an easy process to facilitate Pisanu's wish. It required a staff member situated in front of a walker if Pisanu fell forward. Mike had to lift him from his side and then step behind him. Pisanu then had to grip the handles of the walker with his left hand and his partially paralyzed right hand.

Unsteady but determined, Pisanu stood and with Mike's support, moved forward. He favored his left side and dragged his right foot behind. He grunted, moaned, and grimaced, summoning every ounce of mental and physical strength within him.

"He was going to prove to himself and the world that he was up to the task," Mike remembers.

It was rough going at first. Pisanu's balance and strength were lacking, but like a toddler learning to walk, he gained momentum with each passing day.

"Cheewie Tong Suu!" (We must struggle in life!), Pisanu

shouted across the ward in defiance of the conventional wisdom regarding his fate.

Within a month, Pisanu was doing the impossible—he was walking. It was with the aid of the walker and close monitoring, but his strength and gait had caught up with his determination. Dr. Thomas began calling Mike, "The Saint."

"You have miraculous powers," the doctor said as he watched Pisanu progress from a predominantly horizontal existence, to one in which he viewed the ward as a pedestrian. Mike agreed that it was a miracle but said, "It was him, not me. We just helped him."

Pisanu's joyous struggle prompted a contagious epidemic of hope throughout the hospice.

"Would you help me get up and walk?" became a frequent request from patients who had written themselves off.

Pisanu's health was in relatively good condition after five months of his daily walking regimen. He had shrugged off death since he had consciously chosen to live with his disease rather than wait to die from it. He went further as each week passed, eventually reaching the warm fresh air beyond the doors of the hospice. The threat of quick decline was always present though.

The immigration laws of Thailand required Mike to leave the country every three months to renew his visa. These trips were always a welcome break. By the time his "visa run" was necessary, Mike was exhausted. Spoiling himself with three or four days of rest and distraction allowed him to regenerate.

When Mike left for Malaysia, one fall afternoon in 2005, Pisanu was still making his way around the ward. Mike returned to the temple a week later to see that Pisanu's bed was occupied by another patient.

"Where is Pisanu?" Mike asked one of the staff walking by, hoping he had just been moved.

"He died," the staff member said and then went about her business.

Mike stared at her back as she walked away. He was staggered. With two words, he learned that his friend was now a bag of ashes. Devastated, he sought a more elaborate answer. He would learn that shortly after he had left, Pisanu's gastrointestinal system had failed him due to a common infection anyone with a functioning immune system could have easily overcome. At the temple, gastro-infections were lethal. Within a couple of days, Pisanu was dead.

Pisanu had asked the staff, "Mr. Father—does he know? Is he coming?"

In his last hours, resigned that he would never see Mike again, he told the staff, "Please tell him I love him."

In the days following his return, Mike spent sleepless

nights wishing he had just been given the opportunity to say goodbye to his friend. Hundreds of patients had died since he had started working at the temple, but Pisanu was special. He had given Mike indelible memories of hope and determination. Pisanu was known as "The Walking Inspiration" to his fellow patients. He was an activist for his own cause, overthrowing the regime of despair that had ruled over his heart for seven long years.

Later that year, Mike went on retreat with fellow Maryknollers to southern Thailand. During a break, Mike took a walk through a nearby field. Strolling along a path, an orange and blue butterfly caught Mike's eye. He was mesmerized by the creature's vibrant colors, as it perched on the branch of a shrub.

Intuitively, Mike asked, "Pisanu, is that you?"

To his delight, the butterfly flapped its wings.

Mike concedes that this may seem unbelievable to most. However, he points out that his communication with the butterfly was as unlikely as Pisanu getting out of bed and walking—but both occurred. He also admits, if his colleagues had been walking by while he was talking to the butterfly, they would have institutionalized him.

"Wow, Pisanu," Mike said to his friend, "you look like you're doing pretty good. First you walked. Now you can fly."

MR. FATHER

Mike told Pisanu about the happenings at the temple since he had passed. He then told Pisanu what he had been holding inside for months.

"I'm sorry that I wasn't there for you when you needed me most," Mike said, tears running down his face. "I hope you understand."

Wanting to hold on, Mike realized the precious moment was fleeting.

"Now my friend, it's time to say goodbye. Good luck in your new life. I love you too."

Mike began walking away. He couldn't help but look back. The butterfly was gone. Pisanu was now "The Flying Inspiration."

The first days that patients were dropped off at the temple were the most emotionally difficult. Patients were burdened with overwhelming loneliness. Whenever a new patient arrived, Mike spent extra time talking to them as they wept. Bancha, 33 years-old, was inconsolable when he was first dropped off at the temple by his girlfriend.

"He spent the first week clutching a picture of his nine-year-old son," Mike recalls.

"I'll never see him again," Bancha cried out. "I've lost him forever."

"You don't know that," Mike countered.

Though thousands of patients had died at the temple, the effect of a government sponsored program to provide affordable anti-retroviral drugs (ARV's) had begun to dismantle the belief that diagnosis and death were one and the same. The patients' families may not have accepted them back, but it didn't mean they couldn't start anew. By 2006, there was a group of former patients sharing living space in Bangkok—and working. Mike had no idea if Bancha would survive, but he wasn't lying when he reminded him that his bed wasn't a coffin.

"For the moment you're alive," Mike told him. "If you eat, you will feel better and gain weight. Then you can try these new drugs."

Mike asked Bancha if he could hold the picture of his son. The priest looked at it for a moment, then held it up to Bancha and said, "Can you do this for him?"

"That was all he needed to hear," Mike recalls.

Within two months, Bancha had put on weight, and through a local hospital, obtained anti-retroviral drugs.

"He was determined to get his life back," Mike remembers. "He was on his way out of the temple—alive."

The next step for Bancha was to get a job, but he was hesitant to return to Bangkok. He looked for work in Lopburi while living in a cottage for patients requiring minimal care.

"He was educated, but he wanted to start small," Mike recalls, "so he applied for a job at a gas station. On the application, they asked if he had any health problems. He was honest and told them he was HIV positive, but in good health. They rejected him immediately. He was furious."

"I'm going back to Bangkok!" Bancha told Mike. "I'm going to get a job and when I get my first paycheck, I'm coming back here to take you out to lunch."

Bancha left in January. Mike heard through the grapevine that Bancha had landed a job as a security guard and was living with some former patients. Sitting at the bedside of a patient in March of that year, Mike felt a tap on his shoulder. He turned around and there stood Bancha.

"He had new clothes and looked so healthy," Mike remembers.

Instead of his son's picture, Bancha held up a handful of cash.

"Would you join me for lunch, Mr. Father?"

Mike broke bread with the former patient at a local restaurant.

"Thewada (You are my angel)," Bancha said repeatedly during the meal.

"Miracle," Mike replied.

Bancha informed Mike that he now saw his son regularly. He was also working toward opening his own jewelry business.

Bancha was aware, on weekends, Mike returned to Bangkok to say Mass at the Catholic Cathedral. He asked Mike if he could come visit the church when Mike said Mass the following Sunday.

"He had no idea that it was Easter," Mike recalls.

Bancha sat in the back of the church. When Mass was over, he walked up to Mike.

"This is my first time in a church. It is so beautiful. There is real peace here."

Mike and some other Maryknollers had plans to have an Easter meal at a buffet.

"Now, can I buy *you* lunch?" Mike asked Bancha.

Bancha bowed his head in agreement. Before they began eating, Mike turned to his fellow clergymen at the table and said, "I'd like to introduce you to Bancha — an Easter miracle."

Unlike the many rigors Western religions require of men to enter the clergy, becoming a Buddhist monk in Thailand is relatively simple and in many ways a rite of passage. Like Catholicism, monks vow to remain celibate during their years of service. As in Judaism, monks are required to learn and abide by the ancient precepts of their faith—but to a lesser degree. Doctrine is not central to Buddhism. Buddhists believe over-attachment to form, including the written word, detracts from the transcendency of ethereal truths.

It is common for young men throughout Asia to enter into the monkhood as a means of nurturing a spiritual understanding of the world. Many spend their entire lives as monks, but most return to secular lives after a handful of years. Then, there are occasions when the dying enter into the monkhood, in search of a deeper understanding of the eternal mysteries. Such was the case with Sanan.

"So, I see you're a monk." Mike said to the man dressed in saffron and red garb.

"I am. And I hear you're a Christian," Sanan replied.

After chatting for a few minutes, Sanan said to Mike, "I think we will get along fine Mr. Father. You know—Jesus and Buddha are brothers."

"Yes they are," Mike replied.

Sanan and Mike became spiritual confidantes for the remainder of Sanan's time at the temple. Sanan was quite ill when he and Mike first met, but the monk could still walk. Every afternoon, he held onto Mike's bicep, as the two brothers walked the temple's grounds.

"Those walks with him were so pleasant," Mike

remembers. "He wasn't afraid to die and his outlook was refreshing."

They waxed philosophical about inclusion and acceptance.

"We have both had great teachers guiding us," Sanan told Mike. "Our journeys are difficult, but where would we be without our teachers? No matter what, all religions teach us to be good to one another. That is our common ground."

Every day, Mike listened to patients struggle with the unfairness of their situations. With Sanan, he heard neither fear nor anger regarding his predicament.

"I always tried to remind patients that death may be imminent — maybe tomorrow, maybe next year," Mike recalls, "but that didn't mean we couldn't enjoy each other's company right now. I knew what I was saying was true, but sometimes they just felt like words. My walks with him reassured me that my words held meaning."

From his childhood on, walking had been a solitary and contemplative exercise for Mike. His walks with Sanan allowed for the same peace and clarity to arise.

"It was sacred," Mike recalls. "I felt like we were symbols of the one thing that goes beyond disease, religion or anything else that separates us — compassion."

Their friendship transitioned into memory when Sanan died. Usually when a monk dies, the process of preparing the body for cremation is left to other monks. Yet the monks of the temple had seen the bond that had developed between the two men. In honor of their friendship, they asked Mike if he would take part in the ritual.

Mike began by sponge bathing Sanan's body. He filled the monk's orifices with cotton, so blood would not seep out. He poured fragranced powder over Sanan to negate the smell of decay. Then the monks handed Mike Sanan's freshly washed robes, so the priest could dress his friend for the last time. Sanan was then carried out of the temple and laid in a coffin.

Lighting the candles before his friend's cremation ceremony, Mike harkened back to his time as an altar boy. Chanting with the monks, Mike knew he would always want to serve with the simplicity he had as a boy.

twelve

ROLE REVISITED
PRABHAT NAMPHU TEMPLE – CONTINUED

Access to affordable pharmaceuticals designed to treat HIV/AIDS has been an issue for those suffering from the disease since it reared its ugly face to the world.

In the early 2000s, the World Trade Organization and the United Nations agreed that in the interest of public health, international patents for anti-retroviral drugs (ARV's) should be overridden by countries experiencing epidemic numbers. However, nations choosing to produce generic versions of ARV's put trade relations with the U.S. and the European Union at risk. American and European multinational corporations argued that such actions threatened the preservation of intellectual property rights on all levels. Third world countries, Thailand included, had to negotiate with each pharmaceutical company regarding the lowering of price points for each ARV. Thailand had learned that even *if* negotiations proved fruitful, the medications were often ineffective by the time they reached the masses due to the emergence of drug resistant strains of HIV. Consensus among HIV/AIDS experts has long been that utilizing multi-drug protocols dramatically increases positive treatment outcomes. The Thai Government's decision, in 2003, to implement a policy allowing for the domestic manufacture of numerous generic ARV's as a means of driving down cost for patients was a risky move. Yet 300,000 Thais had died from AIDS since 1984 and over 500,000 were HIV positive by 2003.

As is the case with any sweeping policy reform, affordable ARV's presented new challenges to organizations that had grown accustomed to a dynamic without the drugs. The hospice in Lopburi was not an exception.

The dilemma within the temple involved whether or not the facility would administer ARV's to patients. Contentious discussions took place, as the accessibility of the drugs had an immediate impact on treatment outcomes throughout the country. Dr. Thomas Renard, the hospice's physician, called for change. He could not stand by, watching dead bodies exit the temple while drugs that stunted or even reversed the course of illness were available. He felt to do so would be a breach of the Hippocratic Oath he'd taken upon becoming a doctor. For Dr. Thomas, neglect was as reprehensible as intentionally harming a patient.

In opposition to Dr. Thomas stood the temple's founder, Pra Alongkot, and the hospice's management. They contended that if administration of ARV's in the hospice were to ensue, they would not be able to meet the needs of convalescing patients in large numbers. Alongkot argued that it was the responsibility of hospitals, not his hospice, to deal with a growing AIDS populace being restored to health.

Alongkot's stance appeared contradictory to many. On one hand, he was saying that hospitals should take on recovering patients. While on the other, he had hired a public relations firm to tout the temple as vital to the AIDS crisis. Alongkot had received national recognition for being the face of what was known nationally as, "The Temple of Death." Even after ARV's became a factor in the AIDS equation, he continued to receive millions in donations, much of which came from the tens of thousands of visitors who walked through the temple's hospice each year. He claimed that exposing people to the suffering was an educational tool. Others felt it perpetuated the misconception that AIDS was a death sentence.

After more than four years of unpaid service, Dr. Thomas made the decision to leave the temple. The unwillingness of management to expand the operation's responsibilities played its part. This, compounded by severe depression from witnessing thousands suffer grueling deaths, left him with no other choice. Following the physician's lead, many long-term volunteers chose to leave the hospice as well.

Shortly after his departure, Dr. Thomas released an e-book recounting his time at the temple. Most of the book focused on the doctor's struggles in dealing with death *en masse*, but he also criticized Pra Alongkot's apparent resistance to recognizing a need for change. When word of the book got back to the temple, the few remaining long-term volunteers were asked to leave. Mike was spared.

"I think it was because I was a priest," Mike says. "My feeling was that they would have been too embarrassed to get rid of me."

Although he agreed with Dr. Thomas, Mike didn't feel he had put in enough time to criticize the operation. In addition, the years of stress and frustration that eventually led to Dr. Thomas's breaking point was something Mike could not relate to...yet.

In the following months and years, Mike's workload increased. He was happy though. His purpose was to serve and he was good at it. Patients smiled and yelled out "Mr.

Father" whenever he walked into a room. He fit in.

The novelty of Mike's presence at the temple and the fact that he was one of the few people left that spoke fluent English attracted attention. Westerners who visited the temple were captivated by the anomaly of a Catholic priest serving amongst Buddhists.

"They would ask me who I was." Mike recalls. "When I told them I was a Maryknoll priest, they said, 'Really? A priest in a temple?'"

Mike welcomed the interest at first. He had felt underappreciated during his time at Mercy Centre and in Mae Suay. The pendulum had swung, and for a time, the recognition was satisfying. He saw himself as a bridge between cultures. His discussions with foreign visitors focused on the resilience of the patients.

Mike also had to meet the demands of speaking to journalists who regularly visited the temple. He gave interviews and appeared in pieces by *PBS*, *National Public Radio* and *The Canadian Broadcasting Company*. Pictures and accounts of his work began to sprout up all over the internet. Despite his efforts to shift the focus away from himself, his presence at the temple drew more attention to him than the patients.

"It was becoming all about me," Mike recalls. "The attention was feeding into my ego and I was losing a sense of purpose. I saw how easily someone can be deluded into thinking, *'Yes, I am pretty important.'* I had seen this before in others and didn't like it. Now, I saw it in myself."

After two years at the temple, Mike was proficient enough in his duties to lift his head from time to time, taking notice of the deficiencies Dr. Thomas and others had complained about. The constant flow of visitors became an intrusion. He knew that donations were necessary in sustaining the operation, but the haphazard way in which visitors traipsed through the hospice felt disrespectful.

"It was like a zoo," Mike recalls. "Anyone who gave a donation was allowed to walk through the hospice. They felt like, 'We've given our money, now let's see the animals.' The sickest patients were too weak to walk out or even turn away. They (visitors) asked things like, 'How did you get AIDS?' and 'Were you a sex worker or a drug addict?' They left saying, 'Okay—now I've seen one.' I thought that there must have been a better way to educate people. The hospice was known as 'The Temple of Death.' I wanted people to start seeing it as 'The Temple of Life.'"

Alongkot said, "Patients now feel they can say, 'I am infected. I have AIDS.' So when they have visitors, they can talk to them like they're close friends."

Mike saw the shock in visitors' eyes as they stared at

patients who looked more like cadavers than people. He understood that sympathy brought in money, but from his bedside vantage point, the patients never viewed the visitors as "close friends."

At the end of 2006, Mike made the decision he would leave Thailand in a year. He was beginning to feel surges of discontent regarding his work environment. Service to the dying was a sacred relationship, one that could be easily tarnished if he allowed resentment to take hold. After nine years in Thailand, he wrote to Maryknoll New York, informing them of his desire to serve in Africa.

"I could've stayed for as long as I wanted," Mike says, "but I felt myself becoming entrenched in a role."

In the months leading up to his exit, Mike's discomfort grew. Visitor tours, unresponsive management, and a preoccupation with public relations detracted from the basic needs of patients. Since Dr. Thomas had left two years prior, the temple had not made an effort to replace him. There was only one nurse. The rest of the staff were paid less than a hundred dollars a month—a meager wage, even by Thai standards. Alongkot claimed the temple could not afford a full time doctor or nursing staff despite donations that reached into the millions of dollars each year. It was only during public relations events that Mike ever saw Alongkot in the ward.

Alongkot had spent the early years of the hospice working tirelessly. He had changed bed pans and diapers, and carried thousands of corpses out of the temple. In the late nineties, as the hospice expanded and gained national recognition, Alongkot drifted from caretaking duties to become the temple's ambassador. Mike was not critical of this choice. It was a necessity. Still, he and others felt that Alongkot was disconnected from the daily logistical challenges within the facility, leaving him out of touch with the reason he had founded the hospice in the first place — the patients.

By the fall of 2007, Mike was at his wit's end. When visitors walked through the hospice, he refused to look up and recognize them. Resentment had taken hold. For four years, he had never said a negative word about the hospice to the press. Yet, when a reporter from the *London Times* showed up at the facility, he was unable to withhold criticism.

Mike questioned where all the money was going, as the facility was not required by law to disclose how donations were disseminated. He was critical of the temple's unwillingness to address changes brought about by the accessibility of ARV's. Low wages had led to a lack of accountability, as the staff felt undervalued. Mike told the reporter that staff members often dismissed the needs of patients who had been addicts or sex workers, claiming the patients' misery was the result of karmic retribution. Mike understood the Buddhist notion of one's actions, positive and negative, accumulating over lifetimes. Yet using it as an excuse not to help another human being contradicted the teachings of compassion and living in the present – the foundations of Buddhism.

"I had kept my mouth shut for years," Mike says. "Even when the media noticed these things on their own, I had always shifted the focus away from my opinions. But I was honest when this guy asked me what I thought. I was thinking of the patients, not the image of the hospice."

Mike left Thailand on New Year's Day 2008. Four months later, a story about the temple ran in the Sunday edition of the *London Times*. Mike's statements caused controversy. Alongkot denounced Mike on television and in print, saying the priest's statements strained relations between Buddhists and Catholics in Thailand.

"It was about saving face," Mike says. "He was protecting his image. I think he knew I never meant the temple any harm. I had given four years of my life to the hospice. I am grateful to him, but I had to speak my mind."

thirteen

HELEN'S LAST LESSON
BINGHAMTON – 2008

Mike was given a six month sabbatical by Maryknoll between his departure from Thailand and his assignment to Africa. Whenever he came home, Mike looked forward to verbal sparring with his brother Ted on the topics of religion and politics. Those present found it amusing as the brothers thoroughly enjoyed sticking it to one another.

Mike is a progressive, politically and spiritually. Ted is a conservative and holds traditional beliefs regarding Catholicism. Mike watches *MSNBC*. Ted prefers *Fox News*.

"Welcome to *Cross Fire*. On the left, Father Mike Bassano," Ted said, as the two shared lunch with a friend at the Park Diner in Binghamton.

"Ted thinks I'm a little progressive, but the Church will have to change to meet the needs brought about by globalization."

"A *little* progressive? Yeah right, Mike—change for the sake of change will result in disaster."

By conversation's end, the brothers (and best friends) agreed that their thoughts on religion were secondary to the basic tenets of compassion and understanding their mother had taught them as boys. Ted had not spent his adult life serving the destitute, but he had evolved spiritually from the time he shared a bedroom with Mike on Mill Street.

"I'm not an emotional person by nature," Ted says. "I tend to cling to the intellectual side of myself."

As a young man, Ted pursued a career in accounting. For a time, he worked as a school district business manager and then financial controller at Broome Community College in Binghamton. In 1981, he fell in love with Bonnie Gaylord. The couple exchanged vows a year later. In the mid-eighties, Ted and Bonnie relocated to Scranton, Pennsylvania when a career opportunity presented itself. He struggled with the move. It meant being further away from his daughters from a previous marriage, Gina and Lisa, who lived in Albany, New York. After the move, he saw his daughters on birthdays and holidays, but it never felt like enough. It left him with a sense of inadequacy as a father, an emotional weight that took him years to come to terms with.

Ted worked for a number of universities and colleges in Northeastern Pennsylvania for the next two decades. He and Bonnie eventually settled in Reading, where they raised his third daughter, Maria.

In 2003, Ted was led into his own introspective journey. In December of that year, Bonnie was diagnosed with lung cancer and Ted was told he needed open heart surgery. Ted's operation was a success, but Bonnie died on February 16, 2004. During her last weeks in the hospital, he saw that the nurses on her unit were beset with rudimentary tasks that took time away from the skilled work for which they had been trained. He observed the nurses bounding between rooms, adjusting pillows and fetching drinks. Ted had spent his entire professional life improving efficiency in educational institutions. Frustrated, he told the nursing staff, "Show me where the linen closets are. Tell me where the kitchen is. *I* can do this stuff. I *want* to do this stuff. You do what you do best and I'll take care of everything else."

When Bonnie passed away, Ted found himself at a crossroads.

"I could have gone two ways," Ted recalls. "I could have been bitter because I wasn't there to raise Gina and Lisa, and now the love of my life was gone. But I realized I had a choice. I chose not to be angry. I wanted to do something meaningful, so I started volunteering at the hospital. I thought, '*If I*

could do it for Bonnie, then I could do it for anyone."'
Since Bonnie's passing, Ted has logged over five-hundred hours of filling glasses of water, adjusting the volume on television sets, and doing what he finds most gratifying — talking with patients.

"I realize now that it's all about relationships," Ted says. "Mike has taught me that, but so has life."

There had been an illusion back home that Mike was immune to pain and despair. *"You're the Mother Teresa of the family"* and *"You have been touched by God"* — he'd heard over the years. Many thought Mike was born with gifts beyond themselves. His letters, articles, and conversations always conveyed upbeat messages, where he gave thanks for the life he had been given. He learned to water down stories when he was home, knowing that to most, describing the smell of a burning corpse or the sound of a skull being thumped by a baton didn't inspire.

He was shy about speaking of his own spiritual resolve. Mike's mother had been the foundation of his faith, but in talking about personal struggles, he was more like his father — reserved and private. Sister Margaret, Dan Fagan, Adriano Rojas, and John Flanagan were the select few, privy to the inner-turmoil Mike had dealt with over the years.

His spiritual advisors had helped him define where *The Spirit* was leading him, rather than an image of who he was. Furthermore, Mike's views regarding the Church, once moderate, were now seemingly radical to traditionalists.

"I am a radical," Mike says. "The Latin origin of the word 'radical' means 'to be rooted'. Early Christians were simply called followers of *The Way*. They were the roots of all the overarching structure we see in the Church today. For me, Christianity is a *way* of being. It's compassion. When Christianity or any religion becomes all about laws and regulations, people start to look elsewhere. I understand that there will always be creative tension within the Church and people attached to structure. But growth, on a personal or organizational level, only comes through spiritual liberation. It (growth) occurs when you realize the impermanence of structure and you keep *The Way* alive and relevant. It's *how* you celebrate the Liturgy—how you breathe life into people that makes a difference. I will always stay within the Church because it's always transforming. It's a living entity."

A week before he left for Africa, Mike said his final farewells to friends at a going away party in Binghamton. The next day, he wanted to say goodbye to someone unable to make it to his send off.

MR. FATHER

His intention when he walked into Wilson Memorial Hospital was to visit Anne, an old friend from his early years as a priest. For over a month, Anne had clung to life following a traumatic brain injury from a fall down her front steps. When Mike went to the hospital's information desk, he was pleasantly surprised to hear that Anne had been moved out of the intensive care unit. Mike walked into her room, anxious to see the progress she had made.

"She's in the bathroom," said Barbara Knapik, the niece of a woman occupying the bed adjacent to Anne's.

As he waited, Mike struck up a conversation with the two women. Barbara's Aunt Helen, 99 years old, drifted in and out of lucidity. Yet when Mike told them he was a Catholic priest, the old woman sat up and asked him if he would pray with her. Resting his hand on her brittle shoulder, Mike and Helen recited a *Hail Mary* and an *Our Father*. As Anne came out of the bathroom, Mike blessed Helen on her forehead, telling her that he would keep her in his prayers.

A few hours after Mike left the hospital, Anne's son and Barbara talked as Helen rested.

"So what did she do?" Anne's son asked.

"She taught first grade at Lincoln Elementary for forty years. She never had any children of her own. Her students were her children."

Knowing Mike was a Lincoln Elementary alumnus, Anne's son called the priest. Without hesitation, Mike confirmed that his first-grade teacher had been a woman named Helen Keran.

Neither Mike nor Helen realized their link as they prayed together that day. The last time they had shared a room had been more than fifty years earlier. Mike was a shy little boy. Helen was following her calling to educate children. After decades of travelling the globe in search of answers, Mike had unknowingly brought a few moments of solace to the woman who had taught him how to read and write.

"We never know why we're brought to certain places in our lives," Mike says. "We think we do, but *The Spirit* has other plans for us."

Later that day, Mike took a ride over to the neighborhood of his youth. Standing in front of his boyhood home, he saw himself singing along to the vinyl recordings of Dean Martin and Frank Sinatra. Peering through the front window of Southside Barber Shop, now a beauty salon, Mike could hear his father and Uncle Carmen bantering about the Yankees over the buzz of clippers. Walking down to St. John's, he recalled the despair of being told he would never make it as a priest. As he opened the creaky doors of the church, his mother's pew was empty. Still, he felt the presence of the woman who would forever serve as his spiritual archetype.

In the silence of a spring afternoon, a myriad of memories, some joyous, others somber, surfaced in Mike's mind like the stained glass windows on either side of him. As he stared up, the windows revealed a beauty that, like his life, could only be completely appreciated when viewed from a distance.

Days away from embarking to another continent, Mike was eager to discover new dimensions of faith. He would have to learn a new language and stumble through the nuances of an unfamiliar culture. Creative tension would inevitably arise, subside, and lead him further into the mysteries of the divine. Yet now, with the wisdom service had provided, he would embrace his new life without expectation—just as a child beholds the world as it is.

Afterword

On the Sunday before Labor Day, in 1981, St. Thomas Aquinas Parish in Binghamton celebrated their annual church picnic. The happy occasion saw children tossing water balloons at one another, while the elderly nibbled on homemade desserts.

At one end the of parish's parking lot, a small crowd was urging Mike, a young associate pastor at the time, to get up with his guitar and sing. Mike's affection for music was well known to those in attendance. Every Thursday, he brought his guitar to the parish's grammar school, teaching students songs about Jesus, but always finishing his visit with a rendition of *Herman the Worm*.

Mike submitted to the crowd's calls for him to perform. A fan of folk music, he started by playing a few Peter, Paul, and Mary songs. After he warmed up, he called out for two people in the crowd to join him. Ted, whose specialty was harmonizing, stood to the right side of Mike. To his left, was his younger brother, Paul.

Mike was glowing when he announced to the audience, "Ladies and gentleman...The Cannoli Brothers."

Although he is only mentioned in passing in this book, Paul Bassano was instrumental in Mike's spiritual growth. Two years after Mike's mother passed away, his father died of lung cancer. Born ten years after Mike, Paul was only seventeen at the time and his life was turned upside down. In addition, he was diabetic, a condition he found hard to accept. For the next four years, Paul searched for something to fill the void inside him.

In his early twenties, Paul discovered his own calling as a hospice nurse at Lourdes Hospital in Binghamton. The deaths of his parents and his struggle to accept his medical condition allowed him to connect with the terminally ill. Paul was admired by colleagues for his commitment to his profession. He often came into work on his days off just to visit with those he served, and frequently attended the funerals of patients he had grown close to. Paul didn't live long enough to see both his brothers follow in *his* footsteps. He died in

1993 from complications related to diabetes.

One of Mike's most cherished memories of Paul came on Christmas night in 1982. Mike and Paul roamed the hospice unit at Lourdes Hospital, their guitars in hand. They sang their favorite carols and took requests from patients celebrating the holiday for the last time. Walking out to the hospital parking lot after they had finished, the brothers talked about getting together before the snow thawed. As they hugged one another goodbye, Mike gave his baby brother the biggest compliment he had ever received.

"Paul," Mike said. "You inspire me to be a better priest."

The Latest

Father Mike lives in Kigera, Tanzania. For the last three years, he has remained committed to AIDS sufferers as well as those stricken with leprosy. He has succeeded in taking himself out of the spotlight—literally. Electricity is only available for two hours a day in Kigera. His first six months in Africa were spent learning Kiswahili, a language he found much easier to grasp than Thai. When he arrived in Africa, Tanzanians asked him what tribe he was from, as there are over 120 within the country. He was unsure of how to answer the question at first, but in time, he came up with a suitable reply. He now tells new acquaintances, "I'm Father Mike Bassano. I'm from the Italian-American tribe."

Acknowledgments

Father Mike came into my life in 1978, when I was six-years-old. I met him as he joined in a game of kickball in the parking lot of St. Thomas Aquinas. Prior to that day, my friends and I had always referred to priests by their surnames. After we butchered the pronunciation of Bassano, calling him Father Sossanto, Pinsanti, and Barssini, he said, "Just call me Father Mike."

When I first approached Father Mike about this project, I imagined a book quite different than the one you have just read. I thought it would be easy writing about Binghamton's own "Saint from the Southside." Yet the complexities of Father Mike's life were much more intricate than I anticipated. In researching and writing about him, it was impossible not to look at my own life. Suffice it to say, this experience is one of many gifts Father Mike has given me throughout our friendship. In interviewing him in New Mexico, Binghamton, and Ossining, and then in monthly phone calls to rural Tanzania, he shared with me a level of self-awareness I can only hope to attain in my lifetime.

Ted Bassano provided me with a plethora of information and memories. He is proof that you don't have to get on a plane to serve those in need. Mike's witty aunt, Justine Calabrisi, and his generous cousin, Teri Chapman, brought invaluable perspectives regarding Father Mike's parents and his early life. Padre Mariano Puga and Claudio Escobar lent their recollections of the Pinochet era with remarkable detail. Maryknoll historian, Father Michael Walsh, was a helpful guide in understanding modern mission work. Father Tim Taugher provided me with insight into a lesser known history of activism within the Catholic Church. Victoria Di Savino patiently served as my Spanish translator. Caroline Mewing's precise formatting of the text allowed me to see this as a book for the first time. Cathy Pages' cover design speaks volumes of her talent as a graphic designer.

The following individuals were crucial in piecing together elements of Father Mike's life: Msgr. John Flanagan, Deacon Bill Dischiavo, Jim and Janice Ciancia, Paula Stillitano, Mary Louise Taylor, Barbara Knapik, Gloria Salamida, Mary and

Acknowledgments

Corrado Torrico, Larry Sariti, Tom Crowley, Ruth Gdovin Siver, Clementina Bassano, Maureen Kelly, Ralph Maughan, Father John Putano, James Nachtwey, Kathy Golden, and Gina Wright—with special thanks to Mary Peg Mathis and Mary Kay Torrico (Mike's lifelong friends) for their vivid and insightful memories. To my first, second, third, and fourth draft readers: Kellie Kostek, Kim Hubbard, Brian Chanecka, Ann Chanecka, Mark Toomey, Colleen Mathis, Ernie Savo, Joe Laskoski, Maggie George, Chris Newell, Alina Staicu, Margaret Kane, Joe Zolnowski, and Thom Bouman—thank you. To my advisors: Kim Strong, Tim Mollen, Bryan Ribardo, and Pat Muldowney—I am indebted to you for your honesty, constructive criticism, but most importantly, your encouragement. Liz O'Connor, an incredible musician and person, listened to me read every word of this book over the phone from Key West, unwavering in her support.

My father, Denny McNally, was the smartest man I've ever known. His love of books and history were second to none. Without his example, this book would not have been written.

Lastly, to my wife and best friend, Julie—with all the heavenly characteristics you possess, you could have been a nun. Thank God for me you're not.

Source Materials

The main source of information for *Mr. Father* came from interviews conducted over the last three years. Books, articles, public documents, journals, websites, and multimedia were cited in the text when it did not interrupt the narrative. Some of the sources listed below were not used directly, but provided me with a broader understanding of the political, cultural, and religious contexts that served as the backdrop of Father Mike's life.

Alvarado, Rodrigo. "El Milagro del Teatro Q." *La Nacion.* 26 October 2008. http://www.lanacion.cl/

Barks, Coleman. *The Soul of Rumi.* Harper, 2001.

Barrett, Greg. *The Gospel of Father Joe: Revolutions and Revelations in the Slums of Bangkok.* Jossey-Bass, 2008.

Bassano, Michael. "Rainbow's Promise." *Maryknoll* September 1998.

MR. FATHER

Bassano, Michael. "For the Rest of My Life." *Maryknoll* October 2000.

Bassano, Michael. "From Sorrow to Commitment." *The Catholic Sun* 10 June 1993.

Bassano, Michael. *Personal Journals 2002-2005.*

Bassano, Michael. "The Rhythm of Life." *The Catholic Sun* 4 March 2004.

"Biography: Mariano Puga Vega." *Biblioteca del Congress Nacional.* http://www.dibam.cl/biblioteca_nacional/

Boff, Leonardo and Boff, Clodovis. *Introducing Liberation Theology.* Burns and Oates, 1987.

Briton, Bob. "The Legacy of Pope John Paul II." *Political Affairs* April 2005.

Cavanaugh, William. *Torture and Eucharist: theology, politics, and the body of Christ.* Blackwell, 1998.

Cavendish, James. "Christian Base Communities and Building Democracy: Brazil and Chile." *Sociology of Religion* 55:2 1994.

Cissell, Connie. "Beat of a Different Drummer." *The Catholic Sun* 3 August 2006.

Coles, Robert. *The Call of Service: A Witness to Idealism.* Houghton Mifflin, 1993.

Daniels, Jim. "Go, Tell it on the Mountain." *Maryknoll* October 2001.

DeMott, Stephen. "Gospel on the Street." *Maryknoll* October 1994.

Deshazo, Peter. "Chile: 15 Years of Restored Democracy." *Miami Herald* 11 March 2005.

Durkheim, Karlfried Graf. *The Way of Transformation.* Unwin Paperbacks, 1980.

Golden, Kathy, producer "His Brother's Keeper/Today's Lepers." *Voices of Our World.* 25 November 2007.

Gutierrez, Gustavo. *A Theology of Liberation: History, Politics and Salvation.* Orbis Books, 1973.

Hareyan, Armen. "Efforts to Prevent Tattooing Among Prison Inmates To Curb Spread of HIV." http://examhealth.com

"Thailand AIDS Refuge" http://www.pbs.org/wnet/ religionandethics/

Source Materials

The History of HIV in Thailand." http://www.avert.org/

The History of the Akha Christian Church. http://www.akha.ch// geschichte.htm

Hodge, James and Cooper, Linda. *Disturbing the Peace: The Story of Roy Bourgeois and the Movement to Close the School of the Americas*. Orbis Books, 2007.

Human Rights in Chile (1973-1990). http://www.derechoschile.com/

"I am their family." *Syracuse Post Standard* 30 November 2007.

Kornblugh, Peter. "CIA Acknowledges Ties to Pinochet's Repression." *Chile Documentation Project* September 2000.

Landman, Todd. "Pinochet's Chile: The United States, Human Rights, and International Terrorism. *Human Rights & Human Welfare*. Volume 4 2004.

Llama Surya Das. *Awakening to the Sacred*. Basic Books, 1999.

Levoy, Greg. *Callings: Finding and Following an Authentic Life*. Three Rivers Press, 1997.

Marshall, Andrew. "Is the temple of Buddha's footprints the temple of doom?" *The London Sunday Times* 13 April 2008. http//www.timesonline.co.uk/

Mauchlin, Kerry. "Official government justification and public ARV provision: A comparison of Brazil, Thailand, and South Africa." *Center for Social Science Research*. http://www.aids2031.org/

Monahan, Lynn. "Compassion in the AIDS Temple." *Maryknoll* December 2005.

Mongibeaux, Sofie. "A Christian Saint Living Amongst The Untouchables of Thailand." *Paris Match* 15 February 2008.

Mother Teresa. "It's not our job to convert anyone. That is God's business." As told to Brother John Beeching MM.

Muñoz, Heraldo. *The Dictator's Shadow: Life Under Augusto Pinochet*. Basic Books, 2008.

Ostling, Richard. "Those Beleaguered Maryknollers" *Time* 6 July 1981.

"Padre Mariano Puga Concha: Guillermo de la fe." 11 May 2009. http://revistanos.cl

Perkins, John. *Confessions of an Economic Hit Man*. Penguin, 2004.

MR. FATHER

Radmacher, Mary Anne. *Courage Does Not Always Roar.* Copyright © 2009 Maryanne Radmacher/RedWheelWeiser.com

Ratzinger, Joseph Cardinal and Messori, Vittorio. *The Ratzinger Report: An exclusive interview on the state of the Church.* Ignatius, 1985.

Rettig Report. *Report of the Chilean National Commission on Truth and Reconciliation.* http//www.usip.org

Saint Bonaventure. *The Life of St. Francis of Assisi.* Tan Books and Publishers, 1988.

Selected Poems of Rumi. Dover Publications, 2001.

Thich Nhat Hanh. *Living Buddha Living Christ.* Riverhead Books. 2007.

U.S. Department of State Freedom of Information Act. "Hinchey Report: CIA Activities in Chile." 18 September 2000. http://foia.state.gov

Yo Te Nombre Libertad. Lyrics by Isabel Aldunate.